MADE IN JAPAN

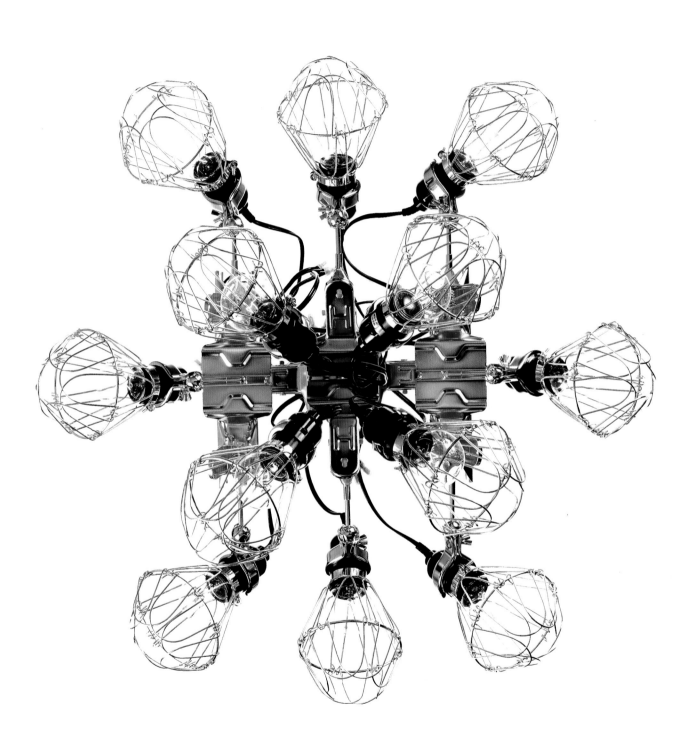

MADE IN JAPAN

100 NEW PRODUCTS

LEARNING
RESOURCES
CENTRE

NAOMI POLLOCK

FOREWORD BY REIKO SUDO

MERRELL

LONDON · NEW YORK

745.2

AR

174430

The entries are listed alphabetically by product name, which appears on the first line of the entry headings. The second line gives the designer's name and, if he or she has one, business name. The third line gives the year in which the product first went into production (or, if the product has not entered production, the year in which the prototype was made). Where the product is marketed by a separate firm, the name of the company is given after the year.

Unless otherwise indicated in the text, all quotations are from interviews with the author.

FOREWORD

I first met Naomi Pollock in the early 1990s, as I remember, when she came to our Nuno store at the Axis Design Center in Roppongi, central Tokyo, and bought a black-and-white double-weave textile. We exchanged only a couple of words at the time, but I was impressed by her penetrating gaze and depth of insight. Only later did I learn that Naomi had studied contemporary Japanese architecture under Hiroshi Hara, then gone on to select various public buildings for the *Japan 2000* exhibition at the Art Institute of Chicago (1998) and publish a photo-compendium of houses by twenty-five Japanese architects. Over time, she became a frequent customer at Nuno; we got to know her taste in textiles and made clothes to suit her, which she always seemed to appreciate. Thus, we often had occasion to share views on Japanese food, pastimes, child-rearing, beliefs, design and architecture, and I always found these conversations very stimulating. Naomi's keen powers of observation, sense of wonder and thoughtful analyses are the very things that seem to have drawn her to search out Japan, as if she had her own unique built-in sensor towards all things Japanese.

One day, Naomi began to talk in a warmly perceptive way about Japanese traditional arts and crafts, folk crafts and manufactured goods, all of which constitute to Japanese thinking the single distinct field of *monozukuri* ('making things'). Many items that were originally tools needed for everyday tasks have become specialized and refined to a degree perhaps unthinkable elsewhere. Naomi quickly set about surveying this vast territory, exploring the full range of Japanese 'products' in order to select exemplary and exceptional designs, from drawing pins and woven straw sandals to mobile phones and vending machines, that would be included in a comprehensive book. Furthermore, she sought out the designers and hands-on makers and, whenever possible, conducted exhaustive interviews.

Not surprisingly, perhaps, even the most cutting-edge contemporary Japanese products, regardless of categories and genres, have something indefinably Japanese about them. Insofar as they are created by our hands and sensibilities, they reflect our Japanese history, environment and culture – although we ourselves often lose sight of such common threads, which are more recognizable from an outsider's perspective. Thanks to this insightful selection compiled by Naomi (who is no longer by any means an 'outsider'), we can begin to see the delineation of 'Japanese form', the shape of what makes our lives, work and play truly Japanese.

Reiko Sudo

INTRODUCTION

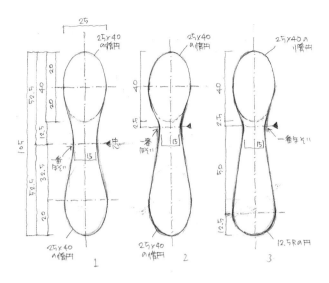

Made in Japan. Today these three simple words connote exceptional design and high-quality manufacture. From household goods and furnishings to electronics, personal accessories and office accoutrements, Japan produces some of the most innovative, elegant, whimsical and well-made products in the world. Created primarily for the Japanese consumer, these objects reflect their environment – the way people live, work and play. They also embody the exquisite craftsmanship and functional perfection that buyers demand and designers in Japan strive for relentlessly. By combining high aesthetic standards with cutting-edge technology, contemporary Japanese product design turns everyday items (such as the humble ice-cream spoon, below) into functional works of art that would look as pleasing in a museum as on the kitchen worktop.

The objects featured in this book have been selected for their ingenuity, beautiful shapes and remarkable fabrication, but they also tell a story of Japan's design heritage, and of Japanese culture in its broadest sense. Encoded in the objects' plastic shells, wooden frames and metal hardware is a wealth not only of historical information but also of aesthetic and philosophic values that are as meaningful now as they were when conceived hundreds of years ago. A close look at these contextual benchmarks will enable a clear understanding and appreciation of Japanese product design today.

In general terms, product design is a creative process that precedes manufacture. Using a series of sketches and models in order to formulate and refine ideas (as in the drawings of the *15.0%* ice-cream spoons above), it attempts to find the optimal physical form for a given function as defined by the designer or client, or both. The process is rarely straightforward, since the forces and priorities that can influence design decisions are almost unlimited.

Designers constantly need to balance potentially conflicting external factors, such as manufacturing methods, availability of materials and cost. Any of these factors can be at odds with the fundamental design values and the guiding principles that individual designers promulgate. Although the goal of product

← The *Chanto*, a series of wooden dishes sealed with sliding plastic lids in fluorescent colours, is a new twist on Japan's traditional stacking food-storage box. It is the product of the Tokyo-based designer Takumi Shimamura (see also *Mizusashi*, page 122, and *Monacca*, page 126), and was launched in 2011.

↑↓ Naoki Terada's initial drawings (above) and models for his *15.0%* ice-cream spoons (2011) led to a trio of mini-scoops called (below, top to bottom) Chocolate, Strawberry and Vanilla. See also page 26.

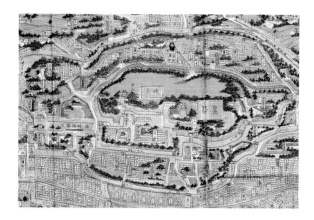

designers everywhere is to create objects that improve daily life, Japan's cultural, social, historical and physical setting make the country's design output truly unique.

CONTEXT

Unlike countries that share borders with their neighbours, Japan is an isolated archipelago stretching from the snowy island of Hokkaido in the north to tropical Okinawa in the south. Most of the population lives on the largest of the five main islands, Honshu; and the heaviest concentration of people living on Honshu is within the greater Tokyo metropolitan area, a relatively flat plain encircled by mountains and sea.

The Imperial Palace roughly marks Tokyo's geographic centre (see top left), and a series of concentric ring roads organizes traffic in and around the city. Yet street grids, waterfronts, green belts and other urban gestures favoured in the West are conspicuously absent. Instead, the city is an organic accretion of small neighbourhoods centred on transportation hubs.

Tokyo neighbourhoods, which tend to contain a mix of residential and commercial properties, are bound together by a web of narrow streets and tiny alleyways (see centre left). Odd stylistic juxtapositions, garish signage and flashing neon compound the visual chaos that characterizes many of the streets (see bottom left). Owing to high population density and land values, individual residential parcels tend to be very small – most homes are 100 sq. m (1076 sq. ft) or less. In Japan, the quality of a space is not associated with its size; in fact, many people prefer smaller homes. Yet most Japanese live with too much 'stuff', and, in contrast to the beautiful images that appear regularly in interiors magazines, clutter runs rampant.

As a result, cramped living quarters are a paramount concern to the designers of objects for the Japanese home. The chronic shortage of space is the inspiration for a constant stream of miniature versions of everything, from cars to kettles, and storage capability frequently drives product design: compact or square forms that fit neatly in a drawer or on a shelf are an immediate plus. But buried beneath the stacks of plastic crates and shelving that many people install to combat the mess lie

↑ This map of Tokyo from 1882 shows the former Edo castle and its surrounding moats. Today the site, which is home to the Imperial Palace (1888), loosely marks the centre of the city.

↓ A city of extremes, Tokyo is characterized by both chaotic commercial arteries, such as the heavily trafficked thoroughfare in the Shinjuku district shown below, and such tiny pedestrian alleyways as the one pictured left, in the Minami Azabu area.

highly efficient floor plans and other space-organizing strategies stemming from traditional architecture.

Interiors featuring traditional straw tatami floor coverings are now somewhat rare in contemporary Japanese dwellings, yet the floor is still more than just a surface for walking on, as it is in the West. Instead, it is regarded as a platform on which daily activity takes place. Nearly everyone removes their shoes before entering the home – a custom initiated hundreds of years ago, when the living space was elevated in order to separate it from dirt-floored areas, such as entrance halls. Low tables and low chairs or floor cushions generate a lifestyle that utilizes space very efficiently by enabling family members to congregate easily, spread out and engage in different activities side-by-side or alter the use of the space entirely by substituting one set of furnishings for another.

Conceptually, the floor, rather than the wall, was one of the defining elements of the historic Japanese home, together with the roof and the column. By the Edo Period (1603–1868), such movable enclosure devices as paper *shoji* screens and wooden *amado* doors were common means of enjoying protection from wind and rain but also access to fresh air and views (see above). Yet the underlying idea of the house interior, a minimally enclosed space in which objects were placed, remained unchanged.

Inside the house, the spare interior was modulated by a continuum of lightweight, movable elements, ranging from architectural fittings and furnishings to everyday items. 'There is a traditional Japanese aesthetic that sees the utmost richness in what is extremely plain. This plainness ... is an infinite flexibility that accepts each and every concept and adjusts to any purpose', wrote the critic and graphic designer Kenya Hara in a book he authored, *Muji* (2010; his *Tatamiza* floor seating is featured on page 192 of this book). While the space could be divided with sliding paper partitions known as *fusuma* and freestanding, multi-panel screens called *byobu*, its function could be transformed by *zabuton* floor cushions, futon mattresses and other smaller items, many of them rotated over the course of the day or with the seasons. Although these elements were light and portable, they had the power to alter the character of a place, as well as movement within it, and they could also be packed away quickly.

↑ Among the historic buildings in Yokohama's renowned Sankei-en garden is the Garden Room, which contains many elements of traditional Japanese architecture. The sliding *shoji* paper screens (far wall, to the left and right of the wooden grille, which is a shading device) have been opened to connect inside and out visually. Various pieces of easily movable furniture, such as the scholar's desk shown here, may be rotated to alter the function of the room.

↑ Handwoven baskets in Japan today, such as this bamboo vessel made by the fifth-generation basket-maker Hayakawa Shokosai, are valued for their refined aesthetics and exquisite craftsmanship.

OBJECTS IN SPACE

This mobility and impermanence of items in the home defines a fundamental relationship between objects and space that still exists in Japan today. In most cases, things that can be brought into a room can be carried out just as easily, especially those used for only a short duration. People routinely adjust their living quarters by adding heaters and humidifiers in winter, fans and *furin* bells to catch the breeze in summer, and many other items of their own choosing every day. And, thanks to the discerning taste of the Japanese consumer, every one of these objects represents a design opportunity.

As regards materials, historically the divide between homes and the objects they contained was less distinct than it is now. Houses as well as everyday objects were made by local craftspeople from paper, wood, bamboo, clay and other readily available materials. As their livelihoods were largely dependent on farming and fishing, people throughout Japan did not have the means or the impetus to travel far. Out of necessity and geographic separation, different regions developed their own architectural styles as well as localized ways of weaving baskets, fashioning pottery vessels and honing wooden tools.

Over time, as the skills required to make these practical tools for living passed from one generation to the next, the objects themselves evolved, some ultimately reaching a very high level of refinement. Basketry, for example, may have begun as a means of transporting fish or fruit but is an art form today, as illustrated by the elegant two-toned vessel shown above. Because of Japan's isolated geographical location, contact with foreign lands was limited, especially during the Edo Period, when the country was all but closed to outsiders. Minimal exposure to external influences generated a certain inward-looking legacy, but it also preserved a purity of thought and technique that is still evident today.

The craft of making things involved more than experience in the use of tools; it required an almost innate sense for materials. Only by approaching them with respect for and an empirical understanding of their physical properties could one coax bamboo to curve, or bring out wood's most beautiful grain. This knowledge was acquired by 'doing', and through the hands. 'The feel of material is related to the deep memory of humankind – like DNA', states the designer and architect Masayuki Kurokawa. 'Like animals, young humans learn through touching. The visual function is not so important.'

Yet even the most utilitarian hoe or iron pot can be very pleasing to the eye. Around the world, the forms of these everyday objects have evolved to match their appointed functions and to fit the hand, not from a pursuit of beauty. But in their efficiency lies visual appeal. Over time and with use, objects often develop smoothed edges or a rich patina; in Japan, this kind of natural ageing is a benchmark of beauty exemplifying *wabi-sabi*, an aesthetic concept incorporating notions of transience and ephemerality that derive from Buddhism.

Refinement and detail were imparted not through applied ornamentation, but through the highlighting of bamboo's swollen nodes, *washi* paper's rough texture and intricate wood joinery. Although these qualities verged on decoration, they were inherent, and often essential, aspects of the object and were conceived in tandem with its overall form. This honest expression of materials seems in some ways simple, but that is deceptive. While the approach conserves material resources, the making of an unadorned form can be a challenge for the artisan, as there are no extra elements to divert attention from the craftsmanship. The subtractive way of making was a difficult achievement that surely required a higher level of skill and perseverance than would be the case with an additive approach. But it took someone outside the craftsworker's world to elevate this approach to a credo.

↓ Sen no Rikyu, portrayed here in a painting by the sixteenth-century artist Tohaku Hasegawa, was one of Japan's greatest tea-ceremony masters. Although he was allied with Japan's ruling class, Rikyu saw beauty in unrefined objects created for daily use, and incorporated them into the tea ceremony.

THE CREDO OF CRAFT

The appreciation of simplicity in craft and its implicit value can be traced back to the great tea-ceremony master, Sen no Rikyu (1522–1591; see right). Under his aegis, the tea ritual became a meditative experience centred on the very mannered preparation, serving and drinking of tea. This sequence of actions included a close observation of the tea accoutrements – earthy hand-moulded *raku* ceramic tea bowls, delicate bamboo utensils and even ordinary vessels that had little monetary value – and the consideration of their artistry. It was Rikyu who first drew attention to the beauty inherent in the plain and the unadorned. From his conceptual spark emerged an aesthetic value that Japan has sustained for centuries.

In the early twentieth century, the products of Japan's anonymous craftsworkers were once again rediscovered, this time by the scholar Soetsu Yanagi (1889–1961), who founded the *mingei*, or folk-art, movement in the 1920s. In common with Sen no Rikyu before him, Yanagi was captivated by the innate beauty of Japan's traditional crafts made by skilled artisans from locally available materials. As the British artist and writer William Morris (1834–1896) had been, Yanagi was concerned about the survival of this heritage in the face of widespread industrialization sweeping his country.

Taking matters into his own hands, Yanagi began to visit kilns and workshops to collect folk art from around the archipelago. Together with his cohorts, Yanagi published extensively on the subject, organized exhibitions and founded the Mingeikan (Japan Folk Crafts Museum) in Tokyo in 1936. His preservation efforts were an important development that launched the revaluation of Japan's indigenous craft aesthetic, but Yanagi had a much broader, and perhaps more lasting, influence by encouraging and supporting artisans to pursue their crafts actively. Over time, his underlying philosophy became the conceptual foundation for scores of craftsworkers and designers who came later – including his own son, Sori Yanagi.

Sori Yanagi (1915–2011) studied art but became one of Japan's most prolific and important product designers. Early on he was influenced by Charlotte Perriand, the French designer who created furniture with the architect Le Corbusier and who in the 1940s was an adviser to the Japanese government on matters related to industrial design. But it was his father's quest for the promotion of craft that became his lifelong mission. 'The inadequacy of industrial production and the importance and superiority of objects made by hand for unpretentious everyday purposes was a constant theme of his father's essays, and looking at the hundreds of everyday objects which resulted from [Sori] Yanagi's six-decade career ... it seems the message was well received', wrote the British designer Jasper Morrison on Designboom.com (January 2012).

↓ Sori Yanagi's simple but iconic *Butterfly Stool* (1956) expressed the dramatic changes he had witnessed in the field of product design, and has had a profound impact on designers around the world.

After establishing his studio, Yanagi Industrial Design Institute, in 1952, the designer went on to create a very broad array of everyday goods that included manhole covers, teapots, cutlery and furniture. Perhaps his most famous work is the *Butterfly Stool* (1956; opposite). Constructed simply from two L-shaped bentwood pieces secured with a metal tie bar, the seat embraced both Japan's craft sensibility and the country's growing technological capability.

JAPAN REBUILDS

Towards the end of Yanagi's life, Japan had become a well-established economic superpower with thriving design industries of all sorts, but when he had started out Japan was still recovering from the Second World War. Product designers had existed in Japan before the war, most of them heavily influenced by the Modernist German Bauhaus school, but the field of design did not really begin to flourish until after 1945.

Following Japan's defeat, American occupying forces arrived in large numbers. To accommodate the needs of its servicemen, the US Army instructed Japanese companies to produce everyday goods, such as electronics, furniture and housewares, to American designs. 'But a lot of equipment made by Japanese companies for the occupation forces spilled over into the Japanese lifestyle', explains Hiroshi Kashiwagi, Professor of Design History at Tokyo's Musashino Art University. This process of adopting foreign products had a big impact on Japanese consumers, and on the manufacture of Japanese goods. 'Two or three years before, America was Japan's enemy, but soon after the Japanese people loved the US lifestyle', says Kashiwagi. Immediately after the war many Japanese could not afford to own their own homes, but as the economy started to improve in the mid-1950s the landscape began to look quite different. To establish standards of quality for new residential construction, the government introduced the 'nLDK' plan system: inspired by Western homes, the new type of layout consisted of a number (n) of discrete bedrooms, plus living (L), dining (D) and kitchen (K) areas.

To match this new floor plan, people wanted modern furnishings, including those described by the interior

↑ Tokyo's Yoyogi National Stadium, designed by Kenzo Tange for the 1964 Olympic Games, showcased the country's technological might and sophisticated aesthetic. These Olympics were the first to be held in Asia.

designer Shigeru Uchida in his book *Japanese Interior Design: Its Cultural Origins* (2007) as 'the three holy treasures': an electric washing machine, a refrigerator and a television. 'But the product design of this period was still crude and unrefined', comments Uchida in the book. 'Rather than the design, the public was concerned with the performance and efficiency of machines.' To meet the growing demand, Japanese companies began to churn out new products, many of them based on American models.

Against this backdrop, designers whose elegant work evoked the spirit of Japanese craft and aesthetics, such as Sori Yanagi, really stood out. The majority of Japan's mass-produced everyday goods at that time were short on creativity and long on mimicry. 'Japanese companies did not have the concept of "copyright" and [freely] used designs similar to those in the US and Europe', asserts Kashiwagi.

The situation did not stagnate for long, however. As Japan's recovery progressed, the value of design, both as an artistic endeavour and as a marketing asset, was increasingly recognized, and design activity developed on multiple fronts. By the mid-1950s a number of design-promoting organizations had been founded, and opportunities for design education had begun to grow. In addition to the formation of design departments within existing universities, specialized institutions, such as Kuwasawa Design School in Tokyo, opened their doors for the first time.

Another major step taken by the Japanese government was the establishment of the Good Design Awards (G-Mark) programme in 1957. It was hoped that, by applauding original design thinking and supporting Japanese creativity, the programme would reduce plagiarism and thereby enhance the appeal of Japanese consumer goods in export markets. Today the programme grants awards to products in a wide range of categories, including architecture and automotive design as well as housewares, electronics and health-care equipment, and the G-Mark designation given to all winning products is still a coveted prize.

By the early 1960s Japan had turned the corner in many ways. The economy was booming, industry was taking off and consumers once again had money to spend. Two major events symbolically marked the end of the period of post-war rebuilding: the 1964 Olympics in Tokyo and the 1970 Expo in Osaka, for which both cities undertook major urban-regeneration projects. In Tokyo this meant building new roads, extending subway lines and constructing spectacular state-of-the-art facilities to host the world's athletes, among them Kenzo Tange's stadium (see opposite).

This prosperity had a profound impact on Japanese product design. 'Since consumers had everything, companies had to come up with new products', says Kashiwagi. 'But they didn't really have an idea of how to do this.' Many different strategies were followed, including miniaturization, electrification and what Kashiwagi calls 'edit design', or combining multiple functions in one object. The groundbreaking Sony Walkman (1979), which combined a small cassette player with headphones, was the ultimate expression of 'edit design', but it also heralded the arrival of Japanese product design as a source of true innovation.

THE BUBBLE PERIOD

By the 1980s design, and especially overseas design, had entered the national consciousness, thanks to growing media attention and Japan's increasing wealth. 'As the economy and access to information grew, we saw rapid globalization and more designs from abroad entering the Japanese market', wrote the product designer Sotaro Miyagi, the creator of *Allround Bowls* (page 34), in 'Design for Better Living' (*Tokyo Art Navigation*, no. 011). This influx had a profound impact on the Japanese design community. Fuelled by disposable income, a frenzy for fashion brands took the country by storm. Suddenly, the latest luxury goods for the person, as well as the home, were readily available. 'At that time our life was totally detached from our tradition', remarks the product designer Tomoko Azumi, who devised the *Twiggy* light (see page 208) and the *Cube* clock (see page 22).

Japanese designers were busy during this period of economic boom, which came to be known as the Bubble Period, but most worked in-house at large companies and very few had practices of their own or were known by name. One notable exception was Shiro Kuramata (1934–1991), who was creating conceptual interiors,

↓ Shiro Kuramata's *How High the Moon* chair (launched in 1986) has the form of an over-stuffed easy chair but is made entirely of nickel-plated steel mesh. A prolific designer of interiors and furniture, Kuramata collaborated with such other internationally renowned designers as Issey Miyake and Ettore Sottsass.

↑ Muji's microwave oven, which is encapsulated in a pure white plastic case with a minimum of buttons and dials, was launched in 1997 for sale in Japan only. Although it has evolved over the years, the appliance's understated aesthetic exemplifies the Muji mission to make everyday goods with a clean appearance that blend easily with any interior decor and lifestyle.

furniture and objects made of acrylic, aluminium pipe, metal mesh and other industrial materials (his steel-mesh *How High the Moon* chair is pictured on page 17). Although the elegance of Kuramata's work was Japanese in spirit, his exaggerated forms and bold colours evoked the postmodernism that was then in vogue worldwide.

To keep up with international trends, many Japanese companies did not just import overseas products but also brought over the designers themselves to create furnishings, and even buildings. 'Japan was like a carnival', comments the product designer Shinichi Sumikawa (whose *Aquarium Dumbbell* is featured on page 42). 'It was an explosion of energy, shape and colours.' Unsurprisingly, the goods that resulted varied in quality, yet all helped to raise awareness of design and underscored its strength as a sales tool.

As if reacting to Japan's growing excesses, Muji, Japan's now famous logo-less brand, opened its first shop in 1983. 'In the 1980s, every rubbish bin had a pattern on it and every towel had a name on it', observes Azumi. 'Muji questioned whether we needed all those patterns and logos.' But Muji was not just a critique; it also offered something unique, and it continues to do so today. Tacitly shunning the luxury market, Muji offers goods that meld effortlessly with the daily lives of ordinary people. Instead of demanding attention with bold shapes and strong colours, Muji products simply blend in (see the microwave oven above); characterized by timelessness and purity of intention, they calmly accommodate to their setting, as if they have always been there.

Muji products are created by a mixture of independent practitioners and in-house designers – all of them anonymous to the consumer – and follow a fairly strict protocol. They are made of neutral materials, such as wood, paper, steel or plastic; they favour clean, simply finished forms devoid of decoration; and they function well. This no-nonsense approach is a direct development of the practical objects created historically in Japan. But at the beginning of the 1990s, when Japan's economic bubble burst, Muji products seemed also to point the way towards the future and were a natural fit with the dawning age of abstinence from the material excess of the 1980s and subsequent retrenchment.

After the bubble deflated, the country had to re-evaluate its priorities, and this led to a renewed appreciation across the design spectrum of things Japanese. Perhaps the prestige of imported goods had worn off, or, more crucially, there was a recognition that Japanese products are better suited to the indigenous lifestyle. Whether as a consequence of economic necessity or a conscious choice, modestly furnished, calm surroundings reflected the national mood.

Most individuals had less money than previously, causing belt-tightening for Japanese manufacturers, too, and many designers found themselves looking for work. Yet in some cases this was by choice. For young practitioners eager to spread their wings, the in-house design department was hardly the place in which to do it. Although working for a company offered potentially terrific training, it also meant putting one's own design agenda on hold, not to mention a lack of acknowledgement for one's contribution. While freelance commissions kept some designers afloat, others entered design competitions in the hope that their idea would catch the attention of a manufacturer that would put it directly into production.

THE TURNING OF THE TIDE

The real turning point for Japanese product design was in the late 1990s, however, when it began to propagate outwards. 'This did not exactly begin with Naoto Fukasawa, but it was Fukasawa who really made the world aware of the originality of Japanese design', says the product designer Tomohiko Hirata, the creator of *Tsuzumi* (page 202), of the pioneering designer, several of whose products are discussed in the following pages (see also right). And once consumers globally had had a taste of these smart, inventive and often beautiful goods, they developed a seemingly insatiable appetite for more.

The attention was not limited to Fukasawa, but his products stood out from the rest and still do. The designer is fortunate in having a variety of outlets for his work: he has an independent practice that collaborates with both Japanese and European manufacturers; he helped to establish the housewares brand Plus Minus Zero; and he works closely with Muji as a member of the

↓ Naoto Fukasawa's *Juice Skin* is a drinks carton covered in a material that has the look and feel of the fruit it contains. It was created in 2004 for an exhibition entitled *Haptic*, which explored the sense of touch. Fukasawa's theoretical project illustrated his 'without thought' concept, and recalled the tactile qualities of many Japanese objects from the past.

company's advisory board. Although each of these groups approaches design from a slightly different perspective, Fukasawa does not stray far from his basic tenet: for him, good design facilitates unconscious human movements that people make, in his words, 'without thought'. 'My design just fits in with the sequence of behaviour', he asserts.

From air purifiers to armchairs, all Fukasawa's products share a spare elegance that has universal appeal, and their crisp appearance harks back to the purity of historical Japanese objects while also expressing Fukasawa's irrefutable logic. The wonder of his realized works, and what distinguishes his products from others on the market, is not that they are extraordinarily inventive; rather, it is the designer's ability to make things that simply belong, as if he had anticipated an unperceived need. Undoubtedly Japan's most influential recent designer, Fukasawa has not only elevated the position of design, but also inspired scores of students and aspiring designers.

In contrast to earlier times, today young designers are coming to the profession from an increasingly wide variety of backgrounds. A degree from an art school or university design department is no longer a basic requirement, nor is it a guarantee of employment at a large company, given the economic climate and changes in the Japanese work environment. While the lion's share of product design is still undertaken by large manufacturers and established design firms, there has been a steady increase in young designers working independently. Although many still cut their teeth in-house, a number are taking their corporate training and running with it, and often they head to studios and offices of their own.

Some young designers hold on to their day jobs but develop products in their spare time for submission to competitions held by manufacturers or others searching for fresh ideas. One of the most established of these events is Toyama Prefecture's annual Product Design Competition, which showcases prototypes by budding talents. Other designers catch the attention of so-called 'design producers', skilled marketeers who ferret out ideas with sales potential, put them into production and then promote the finished goods through their own house brand.

Thanks in large part to the internet, there is also a whole range of self-producers, most of them in their twenties and thirties, who are undertaking all these steps – design, fabrication and sales – on their own. With a few mouse clicks they can trade information with like-minded people, source and buy raw materials, find fabricators and then sell their finished goods via their own websites and online stores. Some of these cottage industrialists cut deals with factories, many of which, when the economy was more robust, had been unwilling to make small quantities of goods.

Other designers, such as Nobuhiro Sato of Pull + Push Products (see *Cement Push Pin*, page 56), make their goods themselves. Part artist and part alchemist, Sato transforms such mundane materials as disposable plastic bags into elegant accessories. Intrigued by plastic's vulnerability to heat, he experimented by melting standard grocery bags. He dropped them into cauldrons of boiling water, tumbled them in clothes dryers, baked them in microwaves, fried them on hotplates and, finally, pressed them with a household iron. Dissatisfied with the results, he switched to rubbish bags, the filmy layers of which turned into a sturdy but pliable material under the iron's heat and pressure (see right).

Sato's first product made from the plastic sacks was a simple, large rectangular bag that he called *PE* (an abbreviation of 'polyethylene'), made from approximately thirty rubbish bags, each of them just a fraction of a millimetre thick. 'If I iron only one layer, the bags melt entirely', explains the designer. Instead he fuses a few at a time, trapping air in between in order to make the plastic pucker. Although Sato uses artificial materials and electrically powered tools, he makes each *PE* bag individually and by hand at his Kyoto atelier.

THE CULT OF *MONOZUKURI*

In many ways, Sato's painstakingly detailed process closely parallels that of a traditional woodworker or ceramicist. But in Japan, even the machine-made and the mass-produced evidence this craftsworker's ethic. This notion, known as *monozukuri* (from *mono*, 'thing', and *zukuri*, 'making'), is as much a mindset as a mode of working. Implicit in *monozukuri* is the heartfelt commitment by the

↓ Under Nobuhiro Sato's iron, ordinary plastic bags turn into a colourful material full of potential. Flat edging strips, melted seams and strappy handles complete the metamorphosis from rubbish bags to the stylish *PE* tote bags that Sato began making in 2009.

↑ Designed to double as a bookend, Tomoko Azumi's *Cube* clock (2010) is heavy enough to hold a row of books in place. Although it resembles a block of richly grained wood, the timepiece is made of cast aluminium – a skill perfected by the clock-maker's parent company, a producer of Buddhist ritual objects for home use. 'For me it was interesting to use their original casting method because this prolongs the life of traditional technology', comments Azumi.

person wielding the chisel or operating the die cutter to do his or her best. This drives the maker to refine, study with the eye and the hand, and refine again, no matter how infinitesimal the change. This cycle of repeated evaluation and revision yields the high-quality products that enjoy a great and enduring appreciation in Japan today.

This value placed on things well made is a source of motivation, satisfaction and pride for the artisan, but it is also increasingly a means of survival for many small or regional manufacturers. In Japan, where discriminating consumers are willing to pay a premium for well-made wares, craftsmanship is an effective tool in fending off the flood of inexpensive goods from overseas or the threat of Japanese competitors setting up shop in foreign countries that offer cheaper labour. Companies are now using design to ratchet up quality, expand businesses and revitalize tired production lines.

For a multitude of manufacturers nationwide, this means collaborating with independent, and often young, designers. 'There aren't that many really new ideas out there', points out Tadamitsu Miyazaki, managing director of metalworking company Takata Lemnos. This is especially true where clocks, some of Takata Lemnos's main products, are concerned. But such products as the *Carved* (see page 52) and Tomoko Azumi's *Cube* clock (left) help the company to maintain its edge.

Azumi had initially envisioned making the *Cube* clock in solid pine, but it is in fact made entirely of aluminium. Getting metal to resemble wood took some experimentation. The designer tried sand-blasting and bead-brushing the silvery surface, but in the end enlisted a model-maker, who painstakingly hand-carved the pattern of irregular concentric lines that is the hallmark of wood. 'If you leave a chunk of wood exposed for a long time, the soft part dries out and sinks but the grain lines remain', notes Azumi. A convincing facsimile of a weathered chunk of timber, the *Cube* clock is a clever metaphor for the passage of time.

It is to be hoped that products as thoughtful as the *Cube* clock will stand the test of time. This is a significant concern in Japan, where merchandise tends to have a very short shelf life – as little as six months for mobile phones, for example. Indeed, it is hard to value goods destined for obsolescence almost as soon as they arrive in the shops. 'Mass-production in Japan has increased mightily. As a result, the importance of things has decreased', laments the product designer Sachiko Suzuki (whose *Bottle*, made from glass vessels destined for recycling, is featured on page 48). But many designers in Japan are trying to make things that customers will treasure and want to keep using.

Longevity is just one of many concerns for environmentally conscious consumers and such design practices as Naruse Inokuma Architects (see *One for All*, page 144). For an exhibition on sustainable materials held at Tokyo's National Museum of Emerging Science and Innovation in 2010, the designers looked to buildings for inspiration. Most timber-frame homes in Japan last for only thirty years, and the materials from which they are made are rarely recycled. 'We realized that after wooden buildings are demolished, most of the waste is burned', says Yuri Naruse. Convinced that there must be a way to reuse the wood, the architects sought out a paper company willing to turn old beams into paper; they then displayed sheets of the recycled product in the museum. In the hope of making an even bigger impact, they made house-shaped sticky notes from the paper, which they called *IE-Tag* (*ie* means 'house' in Japanese).

As in the case of the *IE-Tag*, each individual object featured in this book has a story to tell. Each informs us about the designer's personal taste and priorities, about technological exploration and experimentation in materials, and about the reasons the product came to be. Taken collectively, the objects paint a portrait of Japan today.

On the surface, these products inform us about lifestyle. In the manner of archaeological artefacts, they illustrate how people in Japan eat, sleep, bathe and work. They educate us about their physical surroundings, and they make social agendas manifest. But perhaps most importantly, the objects embody the values inherent in the words 'Made in Japan'. Japan is a country that esteems craft alongside industrial production. Japan is a country in which people take pride in their work. And Japan is a country in which quality matters.

↓ Naruse Inokuma Architects' *IE-Tag* sticky notes (2010) are made from paper recycled from wooden beams and columns salvaged from demolished homes. The architects hoped to find a new use for the old material.

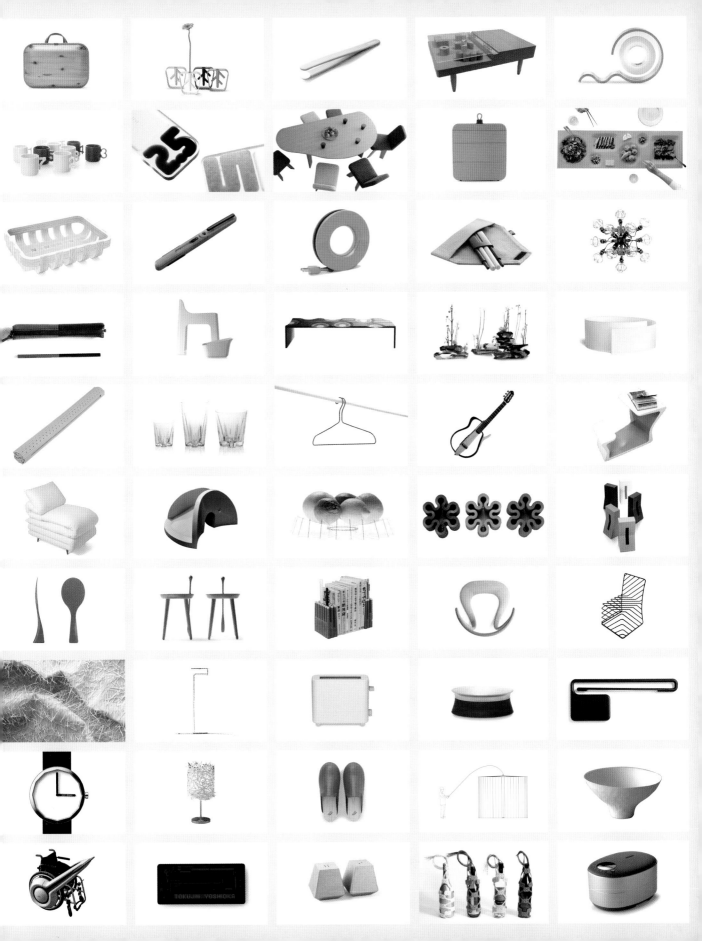

15.0%
Naoki Terada // Teradadesign Architects

2011 // Takata Lemnos

Undoubtedly, the appeal of ice cream transcends national boundaries. But no one likes to have to wait for the frozen treat to soften slightly before it can be eaten. This range of small spoons made of pure, heat-conducting aluminium is ideal for impatient ice-cream enthusiasts. The *15.0%* spoons, which are shaped to fit snugly in the palm, use the hand's warmth to soften rock-hard ice cream into gratifying mouthfuls of velvety confectionary.

Created by the architect, product designer and ice-cream connoisseur Naoki Terada, the spoons take their name from Japan's legally required fat content for ice cream, 15.0%. There are three models in the series: the round-end 'vanilla'; the flatter-end 'chocolate'; and 'strawberry', a hybrid 'spork' (spoon–fork). All are produced by the skilled metalworkers at the Takata Lemnos factory in Toyama Prefecture.

Takata Lemnos, a specialist in the casting of brass and aluminium, commissions many designers to create contemporary goods that utilize the company's traditional techniques. Terada's first collaboration with Takata Lemnos was the *Carved* clock (page 52). This time the firm suggested that he design chopstick rests or a bottle opener, but Terada counter-proposed an object close to his heart. 'I like to eat ice cream a lot', explains the designer with a smile.

Using hand-drawn sketches and plastic foam models, Terada repeatedly refined the design of each spoon. While good balance was essential for the symmetrical 'vanilla' version, the 'chocolate' chisel needed well-defined corners. 'A square shape is better for scraping the bottom of the dish', says Terada knowingly. Using the designer's 3D data, the factory prepares the sand-casting moulds and fills each one with molten aluminium. After a short cooling period, the moulds are opened and the spoons are polished until they glisten.

Just as a cherry-and-whipped-cream topping rounds off an ice cream, clever packaging completes the *15.0%*. 'I did not want the retailer to worry about how to display the spoons', explains Terada. Leaving nothing unexplained, each spoon is packaged temptingly in a paper ice-cream cup, held mid-scoop by a disc of vanilla ice cream-coloured foam. For easy take-away, every spoon goes home in a little cardboard box of its own.

001

15.0%

15.0%

vanilla

01

My Dear Ice Cream Lovers

ACURE
Fumie Shibata // Design Studio S
2010 // Japan Rail East Water Business

When it comes to vending machines, no country tops Japan. According to the Japan Vending Machine Manufacturers Association, in 2010 the country was home to nearly 5 million mechanical dispensers – about one vending machine for every twenty-four people, perhaps the highest concentration in the world. This preponderance is not surprising, given Japan's relatively low crime rate, which means the machines rarely get vandalized, and its big appetite for convenience.

Standing on street corners, on subway platforms and outside supermarkets, vending machines in Japan hawk a remarkable range of goods. Canned drinks comprise the majority, but fresh flowers, ties and a large variety of comestibles are also available around the clock, thanks to the ubiquitous machines. Despite the fact that the selection of merchandise has evolved over time, dispensers had remained largely unchanged for decades. Keen to pilot a new way of selling to consumers on the go, Japan Rail East Water Business (JREWB) turned to the industrial designer Fumie Shibata.

'What they wanted was the next generation of vending machine', says Shibata. Her solution, a sleek silver-and-black steel box with an attached recycling bin created in consultation with Fuji Electric, one of Japan's leading fabricators of vending machines, doles out drinks but also doubles as a marketing tool that records buyer information. Named *Acure* (as in 'a cure' for thirst), the elegant machine contrasts sharply with the usual brightly coloured, attention-grabbing drinks dispenser.

When customers arrive on the platform, the *Acure*'s 47-inch screen greets them with a rolling display of the machine's contents. As the potential buyer approaches, the screen becomes a touch-screen panel depicting the available offerings. Meanwhile, an image-recognition sensor notes the customer's gender, age and beverage preference. Based on this information, the *Acure* makes product recommendations and keeps track of its stock. 'It is not just a machine, it can understand you', says Shibata. It even displays a thank-you message after receiving payment, either with a prepaid train pass or with cash.

The first of these futuristic machines debuted at Japan Rail's Shinagawa station, a busy rail hub in the heart of Tokyo. Slightly larger than most other vending machines, the *Acure* stands on stabilizing steel legs – a feature that stood the machines in good stead even at Sendai station during the Great East Japan Earthquake of March 2011, when they did not topple over. Although temporarily derailed by this disaster, JREWB's plan to install 500 *Acure* machines is expected to zoom ahead.

002

AI WALK
Takano
2011

Going where no health-care equipment-maker has gone before, Takano's *Ai Walk* targets the hale and hearty who need a little help with their bags. An A-shaped aluminium frame on wheels topped with a handle, the *Ai Walk* bears a slight resemblance to a cane or a walker. But instead of supporting body weight, it is a smart-looking alternative to the boxy carts that urban shoppers frequently use to carry purchases home from the supermarket.

Sold in the designer-goods sections of department stores, the *Ai Walk* began as a collaboration between an independent product designer and in-house staff at Takano. Founded in 1941 as a manufacturer of metal springs, Takano has expanded into many new markets over the years. Having identified an unmet need – welfare goods for people who do not yet need welfare goods – the company was determined to create a nicely designed product that would appeal as much to young parents with toddlers in tow as to spry sixty-year-olds. Reasoning that even the energetic find it easier to push heavy bags than to carry them, Takano came up with the *Ai Walk*.

The device's name is a bilingual play on words, sounding like the English 'I walk' and the Japanese 'I love [to] walk' (*ai* means 'love' in Japanese), and its first letter, A, hints at the device's physical form when it is in use. A simple tool with a simple function, the device consists of two aluminium bars hinged together at the top, with knobs on either side to hold shopping bags. Wheels at the bottom of each bar enable smooth rolling movement, and the horizontal grip above doubles as the steering mechanism. A third aluminium piece spans the bars towards the bottom, sliding up and down for opening and closing; with a reassuring click, the bars abut, the wheels fit together and the device comes to a complete stop.

The *Ai Walk*'s triangular shape makes it very stable in its front–back axis, but it can topple to the side when its load is unbalanced. 'We don't recommend it for old people if they need a cane', explains the company founder's granddaughter, Hiroyo Takano. But for everyone else, the *Ai Walk* can be as helpful as an extra pair of hands.

003

AIRVASE
Torafu Architects
2010 // Fukunaga Shikou

In Japan, paper is much more than simply a material on which to write. For centuries it has also been used for making lamps, umbrellas and even sliding doors, and, in the eyes of many Japanese, it remains a material full of potential. The *Airvase* exploits paper's hidden strength. It is bought as a flat sheet but, with a few gentle tugs, grows into a three-dimensional vessel; stretched to a fine, fishnet-like mesh, the vase encapsulates space, yet is so ethereal that it seems practically lighter than … air.

This curious blend of something and nothing is the product of Torafu Architects. The project began with an invitation to participate in an exhibition organized by the group Kami No Kousakujo ('Paper Workshop'). Committed to the development of innovative paper goods, this group pairs the expertise of the paper-printing and -processing company Fukunaga Shikou with graphic, product and architectural designers. Its mission for Torafu Architects was to design a long-use paper item destined for the mass market.

For Torafu founders Koichi Suzuno and Shinya Kamuro, these project requirements were analogous to urban site conditions.

Within this context, the architects were keen to design a freestanding object. The process started with making circular paper shapes and scoring them with short, staggered, concentric cuts that expanded the sheets volumetrically. This labour-intensive task, undertaken entirely by hand, initially took five hours per sheet. But after repeating the process thirty times with different types of paper and incision pattern, the designers settled on using normal printing paper with cuts spaced just 0.9 mm (less than $\frac{1}{16}$ in.) apart. This strategy preserved the material's integrity, increased its elasticity and enabled a self-supporting, basket-like structure.

Using Torafu's specifications, the factory slices paper discs with a press cutter. The sheets are tinted with a different colour on each side, but the colours visually blend into a single tone after the paper mesh is stretched and modelled. Almost as versatile as clay, the paper can hold a variety of shapes – '[*Airvase* has] no function, but we can imagine how to use it', says Suzuno – yet when not filled with bonbons, holding a plant pot or being worn as a hat, the *Airvase* collapses and turns back into a sheet of paper.

004

ALLROUND BOWLS
Sotaro Miyagi // Miyagi Design Office
2004 // Cherry Terrace

Nesting like a set of Russian Matryoshka dolls, the *Allround Bowls* is an astonishing assembly of vessels. Just when you think you have reached the end, there is another one. A thirteen-piece set contained within a stainless-steel basin topped by a plastic lid, it includes just about any bowl-shaped item the Japanese home cook could need.

Designed by Sotaro Miyagi for the kitchenware company Cherry Terrace, the collection is so elegant that it seems a shame to hide it in a cupboard. But creating a product that would be easy to store was one of Cherry Terrace's main goals. 'Since Japanese kitchens tend to be small, we thought an assortment of stackable bowls, including a salad spinner, would be very useful', explains Rikako Iwaki, whose mother launched Cherry Terrace in 1983. Today the company sells both European kitchenware and pieces of its own original design, many of them conceived by Miyagi. A set of French stainless-steel cooking pots that fit nicely inside one another inspired the idea for the nesting bowls. But translating that concept into the appropriate types and sizes of vessels was left to the designer.

To reduce costs, the company sourced a ready-made glass bowl around which Miyagi built the rest of the set. The collection is made mostly of stainless steel by a kitchen-goods manufacturer in Niigata Prefecture, and it has changed very little since it was first released. It includes several sieves and mixing bowls, along with matching lids made of either metal or plastic. Perhaps the most unusual components are a star-shaped insert and matching large plastic strainer. They fit together neatly inside the glass bowl, allowing the serving piece to transform temporarily into a salad spinner.

Clearly, multifunctionality was on Miyagi's mind. While the lids double as preparation plates, the sieves – one of Japan's most commonly used kitchen tools – can be used to wash rice, drain vegetables and make stock. Made of fine steel mesh finished with a flat rim around the edge, the sieves have a delicacy and a level of detail rarely seen in utilitarian cookware. But Miyagi had a reason for this, as he explained in a paper for the Tokyo Art Navigation website: 'Design is about "beauty in use", meaning creating aesthetically pleasing but useful items.'

005

ALTAR FOR ONE GOD
Toshihiko Sakai // Sakai Design Associate
2010

In Japan, where most of the population follows a combination of Shinto and Buddhist belief systems, *kamidana* (small altars for home use, dedicated to one or more Shinto gods) are common fixtures in living rooms nationwide. Perched on a sideboard, shelf or other high place, the traditional *kamidana* resembles a miniature shrine building, complete with steps, doors and a pitched roof. Designed to blend comfortably with contemporary aesthetics, Toshihiko Sakai's *Altar for One God* evokes this traditional spirit but in a highly abstract way.

Sakai's project began with a cold call from a salesman in Yamanashi Prefecture who deals in prefabricated 'house-maker' houses, as they are known in Japan (built by corporate companies rather than conventional carpenters). When his customers moved into their brand-new abodes, many of them wanted an altar to match but were unable to find suitable options at their local Shinto supply shops. Taking a leap of faith, he commissioned Sakai, who earns his living brainstorming about futuristic, 'advanced design' for large electronics firms.

'My basic concept was "don't do too much"', says Sakai. 'I did not want it to look modern at all.' And yet his altar had to meld with today's domestic interiors – a far cry from the wood-and-paper houses typical of the Edo Period (1603–1868), when *kamidana* first gained popularity.

Bowing politely to its antecedents, Sakai's *kamidana* is the product of a skilled woodworker in Nagano Prefecture, who crafts each altar from cypress wood, the traditional *kamidana* material. A plain, upright 29-cm-high (11½ in.) box with a shelf in front, Sakai's version references the rectilinear lines of the historic buildings that once served as models for *kamidana*. Like its precedents, it holds an *ofuda*, a small wooden plaque bought from the neighbourhood shrine (see left).

'We pray every morning to this board, which is connected to the shrine, which is connected to the gods', explains Sakai. 'It is kind of like a mobile phone.' The daily ritual also includes offering sustenance to the gods. Placed on the shelf are small ceramic plates made on the island of Kyushu (where many ceramics-makers are based), in which to put the traditional uncooked rice and salt, and glass beakers to hold sake and sprigs of *sakaki* (a species of camellia). The salt and *sakaki* are intended to ward off evil.

006

AMORFO PREMIUM
Hiroaki Watanabe // Plane
2010 // Iwatani International

Almost every household in Japan has a tabletop cooking unit, a descendant of the *irori*, the sunken cooking hearths that occupied the centre of many traditional homes. The modern versions not only enable the preparation of *sukiyaki*, *shabu-shabu* and *nabe* stews at the table, but also satiate the national appetite for cooking, eating and conversing all at the same time. Gas burners were once fed by a hose connected to a tank outside, but with the advent of the butane-gas canister this dangerous practice all but disappeared. The gas producer Iwatani International introduced its first hose-free cooking stove in 1969, and has been releasing new models ever since.

One of Iwatani's most successful ventures was the *Amorfo*, designed by Motohiro Takagi and Satoshi Sakamoto in 1990. Made of steel, it consisted of a simple rectangular burner with an attached cylinder to hold the butane canister. But after being on the market for years, the design had become a little tired and the technology somewhat outdated. Instead of abandoning the *Amorfo*, Iwatani held a competition for its renewal and awarded the commission to Hiroaki Watanabe, founder of design consultancy Plane.

'I really wanted to make fire beautiful', explains Watanabe. He did not change the stove entirely. Rather, he cleaned up its geometry and simplified its details, squaring off the steel case to improve its looks and ease of maintenance, and covering the folded corners with steel caps; these he integrated into the angled metal supports for the pot. He also replaced the previous flame-generating mechanism with an elegant ring of fire, and redesigned the plastic knob and its graphics to make them stylish and easy to read.

As manufacturing and fuel technology improves, it is likely that the *Amorfo* will need another update in the future. But if Watanabe has his way, his *Amorfo Premium* will be around for at least as long as its predecessor. 'Products often end up as rubbish, but designers have to try to make things that will last a very long time', says Watanabe.

007

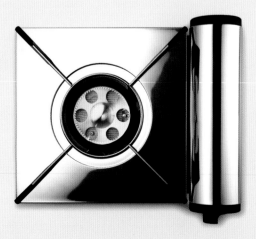

AP STOOL
Shin Azumi // A Studio
2009 // Lapalma

In 1956 the Japanese product designer Sori Yanagi introduced his now famous *Butterfly Stool* (see page 14) to the world. Made of two inverted L-shaped plywood panels secured by a metal rod, the seat was both a feat of engineering and a remarkable demonstration of Japan's craft tradition. Some fifty years later, the *AP Stool* went on the market. An homage to Yanagi's icon, this too is made of bent plywood, but the likeness stops there. Alluding to the Japanese tradition of origami in its sculptural, shell-like form, the *AP Stool* is a single, self-supporting sheet of wood, and its timeless beauty is attainable only with today's technology.

The stool is the creation of Shin Azumi, founder of the design company A Studio, and began as a demonstration piece showcasing the technical skill of a Belgian bentwood-maker; today it is produced by the Italian furniture fabricator Lapalma. Azumi's initial idea was for a stool that could perch on delicate straw tatami mats, a traditional Japanese floor covering, as well as on more durable flooring. This required the distribution of the stool's weight along its base in order to

protect the mats. Azumi thought that, by constructing the seat from a single plywood sheet, he could satisfy this criterion and utilize the manufacturer's skill.

But the geometry Azumi envisioned did not lend itself to conventional drawings or renderings made with computer-aided design. Instead, he developed the idea by creasing a piece of paper, turning it into a freestanding form (below). 'I always like working with paper maquettes because I can understand the shape easily in 3D', explains Azumi.

Azumi's 1:10 model evolved into a full-size cardboard mock-up, which a 3D scanner converted into computer data. 'So the final shape is exactly the same as the paper model I made in the studio', says Azumi. Yet it was not possible literally to translate the paper model into a press-moulded plywood chair. For comfort and utility, Azumi smoothed out sharp creases and, where the folded paper came to a point in the middle, carved a hole that doubles as a handle. Unlike the typical seat, which is concave, the *AP Stool* is convex. 'It is another way of fitting to our bottom', explains Azumi.

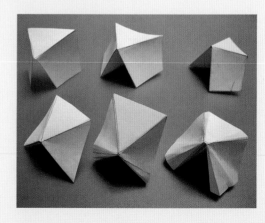

008

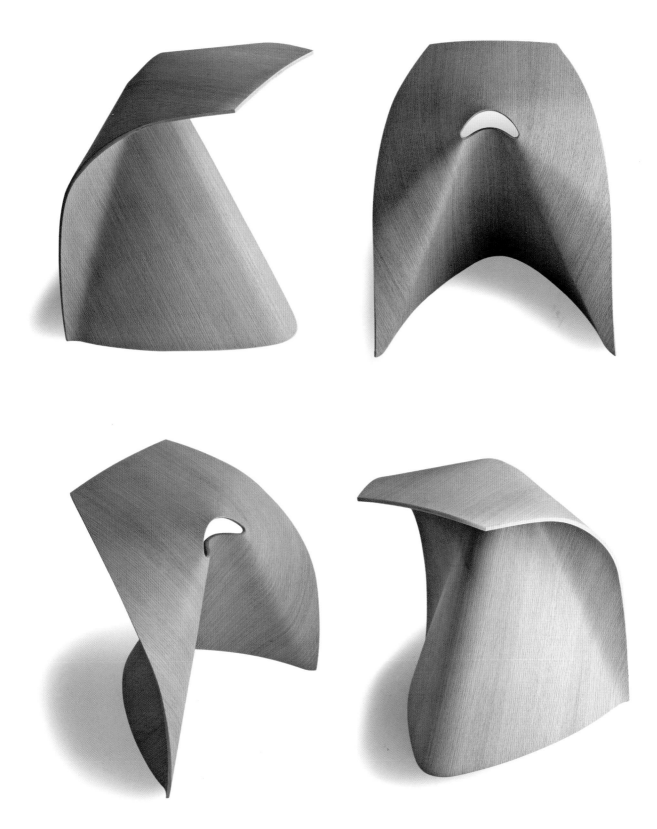

AQUARIUM DUMBBELL
Shinichi Sumikawa // Sumikawa Design
2011 // Takenaka Bronze Works

A sinuous, silvery form that is easily mistaken for a sculpture, the *Aquarium Dumbbell* is more at home in the living room than in the gym. Intended to look good while its owner works at looking good, the elegant free weight was designed by Shinichi Sumikawa and is fashioned in Toyama Prefecture by Takenaka Bronze Works, a producer of Buddhist statuary and supplies. The firm had never made hand-held weights, but it was willing to give Sumikawa's proposal a go in the hope that it would create a new market for its traditional metalworking techniques.

The collaboration between Sumikawa and Takenaka began in the late 1990s with the design of a shoehorn. This was the first product in the *Aquarium* series, an eclectic group of objects with vaguely piscine forms designed by Sumikawa and realized in pure, polished aluminium by Takenaka. Japan's growing interest in exercise and body care gave the designer the idea of adding free weights to the group. 'Most dumbbells on the market are very ugly', laments Sumikawa. 'People need to exercise but it should be a more beautiful experience.'

A regular competitor in marathons who also suspends a punchbag from his studio ceiling and designed Sports Walkmans for the Sony corporation in the United States, Sumikawa thought he could improve on the standard symmetrical dumbbell by reshaping its body and improving its posture. He envisioned an irregular but balanced form with a pointy tip and a flat base that holds the weight upright. 'My image was like a jumping dolphin', he says. Takenaka produced a wooden study model based on his drawings, and he readied the model for production by refining the grip with sandpaper.

Using the same technique as it employs for ritual objects, Takenaka makes a hardened sand mould from the wooden model and fills it with molten aluminium. The cooled hunk of metal is then polished. The weights come in three sizes, ranging from 0.5 kg (1 lb 2 oz) to 2 kg (4 lb 8 oz), but all have the same easy-to-handle shape. 'I pictured people sitting in their living rooms lifting weights', says Sumikawa. But when exercising is done, the *Aquarium Dumbbell* blends in with the decor.

009

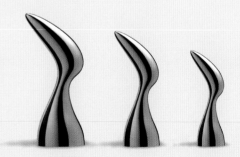

BIND
Satoshi Umeno // Umenodesign
2009

Midway between a book and a newspaper, a glossy magazine can be tough to part with for many people – including the wife of the product designer Satoshi Umeno. After repeatedly knocking over her piles of publications, Umeno knew he had a problem to contend with. But it was nothing that a talented designer couldn't handle; putting his skills to good use, Umeno resolved the matter with the *Bind*, an elegant end table under which the clutter could be tidied away in no time.

Modelled on the bundles of newspapers that people in Japan tie up before recycling, the table consists of a sheet of clear glass supported by steel bands assembled in an X shape that wraps all the way round, like string or rope. While a lamp, book and coffee cup fit comfortably on top, magazines and manga comic books stack neatly underneath, held in place by the steel supports. More than a clever storage solution, the *Bind* turns an eyesore into a point of visual interest. 'Even a messy pile looks good', says Umeno.

Unlike the neat packages of newspapers around which string crosses precisely in the centre, on the *Bind* the steel strips are askew.

The angled arrangement looks more dynamic, but in fact it grew out of an important practical consideration. As Umeno explains, 'the usual, 90-degree configuration made it impossible to slide magazines under the glass', because the spacing between the legs was too small for large publications.

In order to create the necessary gaps, the steel bands cross at sharp angles on both the table's top and bottom. Consequently, where they fold and descend at the edge of the glass tabletop, the horizontal steel strips turn into table legs of different widths – a headache for the manufacturer. According to Umeno, 'The most difficult point was that the width of each leg is different.'

Resolving this geometric conundrum became the bailiwick of the metalworker in Niigata Prefecture who built the *Bind* prototype. For a perfect fit, he cut the steel bars and then welded them together. Once the metal is polished and painted, the joints become invisible, the bars lie completely flat and the *Bind* becomes a multifunctional piece of furniture that is at home even in the tiniest Japanese apartment.

010

BIRD ALARM CLOCK
& Design
2010 // Idea International

The *Bird Alarm Clock* could be described as an ordinary alarm clock, minus the clock. Its primary purpose is to rouse the sleeping from their dreams, which it does by chirping or talking (either in English or in Japanese). It even has a snooze button. The timepiece, which has the silhouette of a standing thrush, does in fact feature a small digital clock, but the electronic display can be hidden from view, allowing the somnolent to awaken peacefully, without the intrusion of ticking seconds and illuminated numbers.

The device was created by & Design as one of twelve prototypes exhibited by the firm at the 100% Design Tokyo trade show in 2005. The collection, which explored the theme of iconographic images, caught the attention of Takenao Shishikura, a director of Idea International, a concern that invents and manufactures lifestyle goods designed by its in-house team as well as by outsiders (see *Bucket*, page 50). 'I found & Design's concepts very clever', says Shishikura. Lena Billmeier, product designer at Idea International, explains that '& Design reduces the product to its simplest and clearest metaphor'.

Arguing that 'clocks are everywhere – on refrigerators, TVs, mobile phones – and it would be nice not to have to see them all the time', Shigenori Ichimura of & Design originally wanted to conceal the clock by mounting the bird on a wall, with the clock side facing the wall. Yet concern that people might be confused by the absence of a visible timekeeper stalled production until 2010. The problem was resolved by providing a 'leg' so that the bird can be freestanding if desired, enabling the clock to go to market.

In keeping with the collection's character, the objects in the series (which includes the *Nekko* vase; see page 128) blur the boundary between two and three dimensions. The *Bird*, for example, is close to life-size in length but less than 2 cm (¾ in.) deep. Encased in pale blue, light brown or pastel-pink plastic, it contains a computer chip programmed to tweet on cue. The bird's 'hind' side holds the speaker, switches, setting buttons and an LCD clock; two batteries reside on the other side, masked by a removable cover. The object's pure avian form disguises its time-telling function, but symbolizes waking up in the morning.

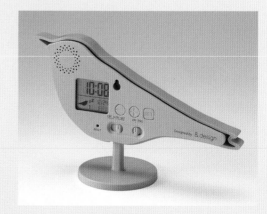

011

46

BOTTLE
Sachiko Suzuki // Schatje Design
2010

One person's rubbish is another's treasure, as the saying goes. Even ordinary glass bottles can have value long after the water, wine or whisky they once contained has been drunk. Using her design skills, the Tokyo-based designer Sachiko Suzuki transforms discarded bottles into beautiful one-off carafes that complement an elegant dining table without erasing all trace of their own humble beginnings.

Suzuki, who has a sculptor's eye, was drawn to the forms of old bottles. 'The shape of a bottle is already complete', she explains. Therefore, her idea was not to start from scratch but to scratch the bottles' surfaces by sandblasting them with patterns. The question was, how to do so?

No stranger to power tools and industrial materials, Suzuki consulted a glass factory in nearby Kanagawa Prefecture. 'I asked, "Can I do this or not?"' she says. Although the company has an expertise in carving ornamental mirrors, the father-and-daughter factory owners were shocked by Suzuki's idea. Over the years they had received a number of unusual requests, but sandblasting bottles that had been destined for the recycling bin? This was a first.

Advice in hand, Suzuki returned to her apartment, converted her kitchen into a studio and got to work. Using specimens collected from a neighbourhood off-licence, contributed by friends or even plucked from rubbish bins, she began by scraping off stubborn labels, removing applied trim and thoroughly cleaning the glass. Once the bottles had been stripped of brand-identifying features, their distinctive shapes and colours really came to light.

Suzuki painstakingly transferred motifs on to the bottles by adhering professional-grade stickers that she had cut precisely into stripes, polka dots and other geometric shapes – some of them quite intricate. 'I was after simple, contemporary designs, not Art Deco', she says. Under the tutelage of the glass-factory owners, Suzuki sandblasted 150 bottles for the product's debut in 2010. She was thrilled when she peeled off the stickers and the patterned glass emerged: 'The contrast between the clear and matt finishes was beautiful.'

Although Suzuki continues to prepare the bottles beforehand and polish them afterwards, she now leaves the sandblasting to the professionals. Branded with a pattern and serial number, each bottle is reborn with a unique identity and valued purpose.

012

BUCKET
Naori Miyazaki
2009 // Idea International

When it comes to heating, the prevailing feeling in Japan is still 'heat the person, not the room'. This attitude, which is deeply rooted in Japanese history, began as the natural response to conditions in traditional homes. Made of wood, clay and paper, houses tended to be under-insulated and very draughty, especially in the dead of winter when temperatures can drop well below freezing in parts of the archipelago.

Localized sources of heat, such as *irori* sunken cooking hearths and *hibachi* 'fire bowl' burners, helped to counter this problem in the past. More recently, kerosene stoves, electric wall units and *kotatsu* tables with plug-in heating elements on the underside have taken over the job. But in the typical Japanese home, in which central heating is a rarity, this piecemeal approach often leaves toes and other extremities out in the cold. The *Bucket*, a portable personal heater made by lifestyle-products developer Idea International (see also page 46), was designed to solve this problem.

The *Bucket* is modelled in the shape of a rectangular pail, and has a handle that enables easy carrying but also acts as a stand, directing the heater's louvred front upwards.

Inside, electricity-fed ceramic strips heat the air as a motorized fan blows it outwards. Should the *Bucket* be knocked, the louvres automatically shut, the current cuts out and the heater turns off. When not in use, the compact appliance fits comfortably on a shelf.

Although portability and storage potential were key considerations, the *Bucket*'s size was largely determined by the space required for the heating element. After selecting the ceramic unit from the Chinese manufacturer's available models, Naori Miyazaki, an in-house designer at Idea International, configured and coloured the boxy shell. Betting on the power of suggestion, Miyazaki went for warm hues – red, orange and brown – in addition to the perennial favourite, white. 'We tend not to use vivid colours', he explains. 'Since it is easy to match, white is very popular.'

Blending easily with most Japanese kitchens and bathrooms (where body parts are most often exposed), the *Bucket* concentrates warmth where it is needed most while keeping electricity usage down – a greater concern than ever in the energy-saving climate resulting from the Great East Japan Earthquake of March 2011.

013

CARVED
Naoki Terada // Teradadesign Architects
2010 // Takata Lemnos

The *Carved* is a white wall clock that can literally blend into the background. Against a white wall, its colour is practically indistinguishable, and the slightly rough texture of its round face appears to be the product of a paint roller. Although incised numbers and surface-mounted hands set it apart from the wall, the *Carved* seems closer to the building itself than to its furnishings.

Unsurprisingly, the clock is the product of an architect, Naoki Terada. The *Carved* began when he was designing a house in suburban Tokyo for his sister and her family. Terada did not stop at creating only the building: 'I wanted to coordinate everything, down to the cutlery', he says. Fortunately his were willing clients, and metalworking company Takata Lemnos was eager to put the clock into production.

Takata Lemnos had collaborated with product designers before, but was keen to update its work and this time wanted an architect's point of view. Taking his cue from the effect of the sun's daily cycle on walls and rooms, Terada used the play of light and shadow to articulate the clock's deeply grooved numbers. Conveniently, the clock's face is especially legible in the morning, when the sun is low – and everybody is pressed for time.

Numerals (either Roman or Arabic) or simple tick marks, etched into the artificial-wood surface with a computerized drill, abut the edge of the clock face. Each digit is cut off at the top or bottom, leaving the imagination to round out the '8' or top off the '2'. This has resonance in Japan, where traditional artists often omit lines or crop images. Although small, this important detail also makes the numbers visible from both the side and below. 'I thought it would be interesting to see the numbers in section', Terada explains.

The three different fonts devised for the clock, all designed by the architect, have a clean, timeless quality. But the numbers' precise shapes, their rounded corners and widths, were determined by the drill bit. While it took the expertise of a woodworking factory in Hokkaido to handle the carving, Takata Lemnos left its mark on the clock's hands: although painted white to match, they are made of stainless steel.

014

CD PLAYER
Naoto Fukasawa
2004 // Muji

Inspiration from a wall-mounted ventilation fan led the product designer Naoto Fukasawa to design this CD player, which became his breakthrough product. Although it started out as a conceptual prototype created for an exhibition, it ended up as a bestseller in Muji shops around the world. It is compact and easy to operate, so it is no surprise that people love it; but its real strength is the ingenious way in which it trades the conventional player's shape for a form with more meaning.

CD players, those devices that brought about the slow death of the record player, enjoyed their time in the sun before the arrival of the MP3 player. Freed from the need to hold large vinyl LPs, the standard-issue 'compact disc' unit was a nondescript thin black box that mysteriously swallowed CDs and emitted music. Not only did it lack an iconic shape, but also there was no particular connection between the machine's appearance and its function. 'People did not really recognize it as a CD player', explains Fukasawa. But in the movement and straightforward shape of the ventilation fan, Fukasawa saw a form beautifully suited to the CD player's purpose.

Borrowing the geometry of the fan – a circle inscribed in a square – Fukasawa created a small CD player with an exposed disc in the centre rimmed by speakers built into the frame. Activated via a pull-cord that doubles as the player's electricity supply line, the spinning disc mimics the rotation of a fan's blades but releases sound waves instead of air currents. The CD's movement, which in conventional players is not visible, offers a physical expression of the sound emanating from the speakers.

Fukasawa introduced his initial concept at an exhibition in Tokyo that featured items created for his first 'Without Thought' workshop, which explored the process of designing objects so naturally suited to daily life that people would use them without thinking. Intrigued by Fukasawa's idea, the head of Muji's product development team agreed to turn the prototype player into a product. 'It was so unique and different, only Muji could make it', says Fukasawa. But as in the case of all Muji merchandise, his CD player fits effortlessly into people's lives. In the words of its designer, it is used 'without thinking'.

015

CEMENT PUSH PIN
Nobuhiro Sato // Pull + Push Products
2003

In common with legions of Kyoto craftsmen before him, Nobuhiro Sato plies his trade with precision and attention to detail. But instead of working with wood, bamboo or clay, Sato uses a 'palette' of assorted materials procured at home superstores, and instead of crafting traditional objects, he produces tote bags from plastic bags (see page 21) and objects of daily use from cement.

Sato's first foray into working with cement was to make incense burners, which he modelled in the shape of miniature houses and sold at local flea markets. 'I thought it would be interesting to use an exterior material for interior goods', he reasons. Keen to expand his line, Sato soon added coasters, ashtrays and pushpins (large-headed drawing pins) to his line of goods.

The designer enjoyed moulding household items from construction-grade masonry, but also the inherent play on scale. Normally used for buildings and other large projects, cement takes on a different character when presented in small pieces, according to Sato. 'It is visually more interesting', he explains. And among Sato's works, none underscores this contrast more sharply than the tiny pushpin.

Sato's pushpin production began with an investigation of the curing technology used at concrete-block factories. 'At first I had no idea what I was doing', he admits. Yet an arduous process of trial and error led to his sure-fire but labour-intensive method, which involves using ice-cube trays in order to mould 180 pieces at a time.

The most painstaking step is positioning the pins before the concrete sets: they must be perfectly vertical and precisely centred within their respective cubes. Once the concrete has hardened, Sato removes the pushpins from the moulds and finishes each one by hand. For variation, before the pouring stage he places in the bottom of each mould some tiny stones usually used in aquariums; he later brushes off some cement to achieve a pebbly surface – a trick borrowed from traditional Japanese masons.

No pushpin is complete until it has been properly cured for a week in a plastic bag. 'If they dry too quickly, they do not develop strength', Sato explains. Owing to flaws that appear during the production and curing processes, a quarter of each batch never makes it to market. But the rest bring out cement's surprising inner beauty.

016

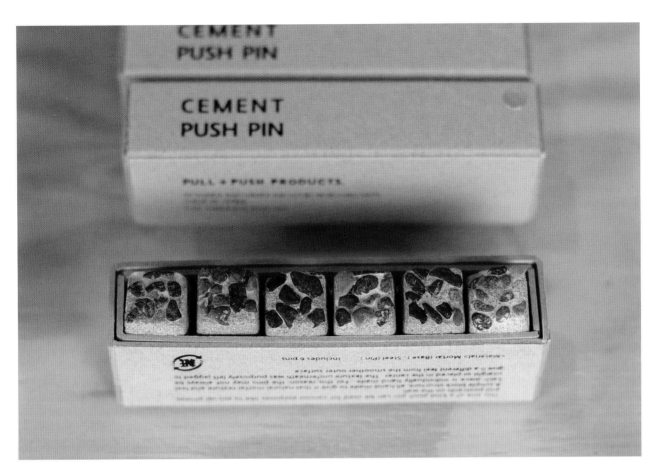

CEMENT
PUSH PIN

CEMENT
PUSH PIN

PULL + PUSH PRODUCTS

Material: Mortar (Base), Steel (Pin)   Includes 6 pins

CHIBION TOUCH
Satoshi Nakagawa // Tripod Design
2011 // Pigeon Corporation

No matter the country, many children around the world hate to have their temperature taken. But in Japan, a lot of youngsters are regularly subjected to this ordeal, especially those enrolled in government-funded nurseries and kindergartens. The thermometer is a quick means of identifying sick children before they leave home for the day, and thus acts as a first line of defence against spreading colds and other illnesses.

In Japan, temperature is most commonly measured by placing a conventional long, thin thermometer in a closed underarm, a painless procedure that nevertheless often elicits tears, fear and other adverse reactions from children. When the designer Satoshi Nakagawa was asked by the Pigeon Corporation, a manufacturer of childcare and women's health products, to create an updated temperature monitor, he thought he had better get to the root of the problem first.

For Nakagawa, this entailed direct observation of mothers taking their children's temperatures, during which he noted the parents' gestures and postures as well as the reactions of the young ones. To gain an even better understanding of a child's perspective, Nakagawa made a model with small cameras in place of eyes in order to simulate a baby's vision. 'We felt that the children were frightened by the thermometer itself – it's shiny and needle-like', explains the designer.

Reflecting on the medical instruments of his own youth, Nakagawa recalled stethoscopes with cup-shaped chest pieces that were neither sharp nor scary. Inspired by this form, he made a series of round or bell-shaped prototypes and asked mothers to test them by placing them on their children's foreheads. This time the reaction was totally different. Instead of assuming an aggressive stance of aiming a thermometer at an underarm, the mothers maintained a gentle and nurturing body language. And, faced with calm, unfazed mothers, the children did not cry or appear to be frightened; to them, the circular thermometer was no more threatening than the feel of their mother's hands.

Made of plastic and rubber, the *Chibion Touch* is both comfortable on the skin and, with a diameter of 4.7 cm (just under 2 in.), easy for a parent to hold and use, even on a sleeping baby. The simple, battery-powered device calculates in a matter of seconds the child's body temperature, based on those of the skin's surface and the ambient air, and quietly displays the result.

017

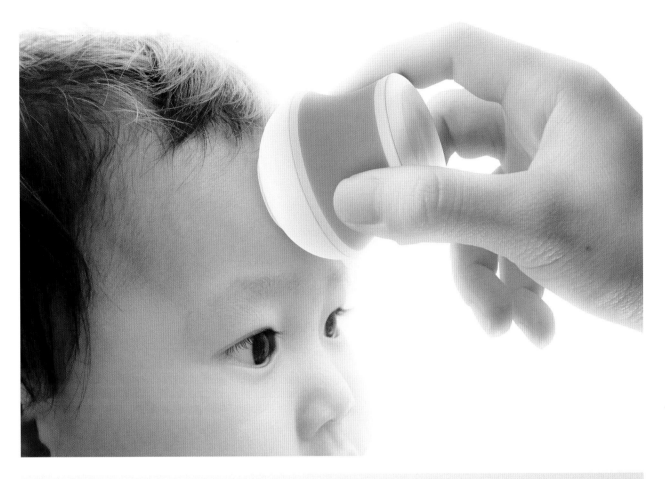

CONOF. SHREDDER
Color
2008 // Silver Seiko

Although it is the shape and size of a rubbish bin, this shredder could not be confused with a garbage disposal device, even a very smart one. While most of its counterparts are utilitarian appliances that one would want to store out of sight, this elegant tapered tub – which slices almost noiselessly through CDs, DVDs and computer disks as well as paper – is as easy on the eye as it is on the ears. Even the diamond-shaped cuttings it produces are aesthetically pleasing.

The *Conof. Shredder* was created by Color, a design firm founded by a Tokyo-based trio with experience in product, graphic and space design. Mindful of the visual cacophony that plagues people in Japan daily, the trio combine their skills to produce goods for the home and office that have an understated appearance and an easily understood function. 'Our theme is "comfortable atmosphere"', says Color's Akiko Shirasu.

It took some ingenuity to apply that principle to the design of the shredder Color generated for Silver Seiko, an appliance manufacturer in Niigata Prefecture. In contrast to the usual sharp-edged box littered with gizmos and gadgets, the design firm created an uncomplicated, wedge-shaped black box to hold the cutting mechanism – which contains separate rolling blades for paper and disks – and sat it neatly in a splayed receptacle for waste matter. The composite form may look simple, but it took six months to perfect the crisp line where top and receptacle meet. 'Ordinary people may not notice this edge, but unconsciously it makes the design "comfortable"', explains Color's Noriyuki Shirasu. Rounded corners and a range of gentle colours add to the soft overall appearance.

Much thought was also given to the concise graphics, which convey only the necessary information. 'Usually the graphic designer is different from the product designer, so there are lots of bad graphics out there', laments Noriyuki, who prides himself on designing each product from initial concept to final package. On the *Conof. Shredder* a row of illustrations, printed along the edge of the black top, guides users regardless of their native tongue, and figural icons remind people not to catch their hair or fingers in the cutters. A sliding button controls the direction of the paper feed, enabling a quick reversal if an important form mistakenly ends up in the intake slot.

018

COOK ONE
Hideo Yamamoto // Ottimo Design
2004 // Namsun

In Japan, where few kitchens have Western-style gas or electric ovens, most people prepare their meals on a grill or hob. Catering to these cooking methods is a whole panoply of pots and pans intended for direct exposure to high heat. The *Cook One* frying pan, which appears to be made of cast iron but is in fact aluminium, can stand up to the heat challenge without compromising its classic good looks.

This no-nonsense pan is the product of Hideo Yamamoto, who has designed numerous household items, including a humidifier, a toilet brush and a vacuum cleaner (all for Muji, Japan's perennially popular purveyor of plain but beautifully formed products for the home). The *Cook One* was commissioned by a now defunct aluminium manufacturer; today it is manufactured in Korea but marketed in Japan.

Unlike inexpensive cookware made from pressed-metal plates, the *Cook One* is made of die-cast aluminium, enabling Yamamoto to fine-tune the thickness of the pan. To ensure an even and controlled distribution of heat, the hefty bottom is considerably thicker than the sides; yet, because of its aluminium construction, the pan remains lightweight and easy to carry.

The handle, which is attached to the pan with a concealed screw on its underside, blends seamlessly with the aluminium body but is made of plastic. As Yamamoto says, the pan 'has the look of a professional frying pan', but the home cook will not need to reach for a tea towel or oven gloves when faced with lifting a hot *Cook One*. To cut down on material, and therefore weight, the handle is hollowed out down its length, creating a shallow trough that conveniently doubles as a rest for chopsticks or a mixing spoon.

The surface of the *Cook One* pan was originally coated with Teflon, but after concerns arose about health risks associated with that smooth resin the manufacturer switched to a non-stick ceramic finish. Both the pan and the handle are tinted black, so are not likely to become stained or discoloured, ensuring that the *Cook One* maintains its appearance and utility for a long time.

019

COOKI
Toshiyuki Kita // IDK Design Laboratory
2008 // Stile Life

Japan has a culture of hot water. Many people start their day with freshly brewed green tea and end it with a long soak in a deep bath, and in kitchens nationwide electric hot-water heaters occupy a place of honour, ensuring that a warm drink is always at the ready. But Toshiyuki Kita's *Cooki* kettle harks back to a time when everyone heated water on a burner; although its seamless construction is the product of today's technology, its classic good looks are timeless.

The *Cooki*'s streamlined stainless-steel surface bows politely to international mid-twentieth-century Modernism, but the pleasing pairing of round pot and arched handle evokes the form of traditional Japanese tea kettles, which were made of iron. 'In the past, purely decorative elements were scarce in Japan', explains Kita; instead, beauty emerged naturally when function and form evolved in tandem. Thinking with his pencil, Kita began his own blending of form and function with a hand-drawn sketch, but he advanced quickly to 3D models, which enabled him to refine the kettle's shape and test its utility. The end product is a safe, user-friendly kettle that even elderly people – a growing proportion of Japan's population – can handle comfortably.

The pot, which has a capacity of 2.6 litres (about 4½ pints), is slightly squat, so that it sits stably on both electric and gas stove tops. Its steel shell yields high thermal efficiency and, mindful of his customers' hands, Kita folded all sharp metal edges inward. Intended not just to boil water but also to brew the medicinal herb teas commonly prescribed in Japan, the *Cooki* has an exceptionally wide lid with a pretty leaf-shaped knob that was designed specifically to be easy to grasp. To ensure that the hot liquid reaches the cup safely, Kita devised a non-drip spout and a thick, easy-grip, non-slip resin handle that makes tilting the kettle nearly effortless.

020

EDOKOMON
Nikko
2003

Sized for holding sashimi and soba noodles, the *Edokomon* plates and bowls by the ceramics-maker Nikko cater to Japanese taste. But their elegant shapes and intricate patterns would satisfy anyone with a yen for beautiful tableware. The collection takes its name – as well as its charming blue-and-white designs – from the miniature motifs (*komon*) that decorated undergarments worn by the ruling Samurai class during the Edo Period (1603–1868). The stylized patterns were reborn as porcelain glaze in 2003, and are the perfect decoration for the dishes' smooth surfaces.

The *Edokomon* line, which was introduced in honour of the 400th anniversary of the beginning of the Edo Period, is one of the few Japanese styles produced by Nikko. Founded in 1908, the company initially specialized in Western dinner sets, a large portion of them for export, but began making dishes for Japanese cuisine after the country's 'bubble economy' burst in the 1990s.

Following the earlier period of vigorous, money-driven internationalization, the enjoyment of Japanese culture and lifestyle came back into vogue. 'It gave us the chance to appreciate what we have again', explains Nikko's managing officer, Koshiro Sambai. And food was no exception. Feeding this trend, the *Edokomon* tableware collection started with delicate square plates and small bowls to hold the individual portions typically eaten at the Japanese table. 'Japanese dishes are naturally a different size, because the furniture and people are smaller', says Sambai. Yet the collection has grown to include pieces suitable for fusion cuisine, as well as round types for Western menus.

All the pieces are adorned with one of seven decal or relief patterns rendered in a tinted glaze of cobalt blue or celadon (a pale grey–green), colours that have been associated with Asian crockery for centuries. The patterns – subtle reinterpretations of antique designs inspired by nature – were created at Nikko's headquarters in Ishikawa Prefecture by a team of fifteen designers. Each design is composed of either tiny squares or dots that coat the entire dish: some resemble fish scales or spiralling eddies, others evoke cherry blossoms or clusters of irises. Abstract and geometric, all the motifs look remarkably modern, and each is a feast for the eye.

021

F,L,O,W,E,R,S
Norihiko Terayama // Studio Note
2007

Most rulers are intended to measure objects, but the *F,l,o,w,e,r,s* performs this task with unparalleled delicacy. Designed and produced by Norihiko Terayama, this metric ruler is a simple bar of clear acrylic that preserves a row of red flowers spaced precisely 1 cm (⅜ in.) apart: the twenty-eight stems are an accurate gauge, while the tiny blooms add a decorative touch to the desk.

The project began shortly after Terayama returned to Japan following a four-year stint studying and working in The Netherlands. Since he did not have a job, the designer enjoyed walking his dog and taking in the scenery. In particular, random clusters of flowers caught his attention. 'A flower has no inherent function [as a tool]', says Terayama. 'But I thought it was interesting that flowers could acquire a function if lined up.' They could even become a means of measurement.

Inspired by these observations, Terayama began making rulers, using red-tinged flowers. Although he had a soft spot for these blooms, they were too big to fit comfortably inside the oblong acrylic strip. But baby's breath (*Gypsophila*) was an appealing substitute that was readily available in the desired quantity at several florists' within easy cycling distance of his home studio; Terayama buys up to 300 sprigs at a time.

Making the fresh blooms ruler-ready, however, is an arduous process. In addition to dyeing the white petals to match the original red ones, Terayama must dry the plants in floral desiccant powder. 'Water left inside the flowers will make bubbles in the acrylic', he explains. Using tweezers, he painstakingly straightens, positions and glues each brittle stem to a sheet of acrylic. A narrow band at the bottom, notched with 1 cm increments, guides the flowers' placement but is removed at the end. This assembly then goes to Saitama Prefecture, where an acrylic expert sands and trims the blossom-bedecked board, and finally tops it with his signature clear material.

The finished product has the proportions of a standard ruler, measuring 30 x 4 cm (just under 12 x 1½ in.). But its 0.9-cm (just under ⅜ in.) depth enables the flowers to stand up straight and look delightful.

022

FELT HOOK
Furnish
2010

Landlords often get grumpy with tenants who poke holes in their walls. But that did not stop Furnish, a Tokyo-based trio of designers, from inventing the *Felt Hook*. A wall-mounted coat hook formed in the shape of a candleholder but made of matted fibres, it is both fun and functional.

Furnish principal Satoshi Yoshikawa got the idea for the *Felt Hook* while he was in London to participate in a design exhibition. After observing wall-hung works displayed by other designers, he decided to make a wall-mounted hook, but not just any old hook: its design had to be clever and its manufacture easy. Although he was inspired by lanterns and cantilevered light fixtures from London's historic buildings, he modelled the hook on an appropriately interior candlestick instead.

Back in Tokyo, Yoshikawa resolved the design of the hook in a few months, then moved smoothly into Furnish's usual self-production mode. In common with many Furnish products, the hook is made of industrial-grade polyester felt. 'Wood, metal and plastic require sophisticated technology, so we wanted a different material that is easier to work with, attractive and useful', explains Yoshikawa. Through his father, who was in the stuffed-toy business, the designer met a wholesale felt producer in Tokyo who was willing to sell to such a small outfit as Furnish.

Zipping around in his Honda Civic, Yoshikawa transported the felt from the manufacturer to the die cutter, where technicians cut the 1-cm-thick (⅜ in.) pad into the *Felt Hook*'s three pieces: the candlestick, plus two oval disks for stability. Back at Furnish headquarters, the designers sealed the felt parts, plus necessary screws and other metal hardware and instructions, into their vacuum packages.

For the consumer, installing the *Felt Hook* is easy; all it takes is a screwdriver and a little elbow grease. Since the hook is made from hard, heat-pressed polyester, it is strong enough to support up to 2.5 kg (5 lb 8 oz). Although it has the outline of a burning candle, it is, paradoxically, weak in the face of intense heat. 'It is kind of a joke', laughs Yoshikawa. But on a more serious note, amusement is an important attribute of Furnish products. As the designer states, 'I do not want to just make simple things, but ones with humour.'

023

FUJIYAMA GLASS
Keita Suzuki
2010 // Sugahara Glassworks

A snow-capped peak rising majestically some 60 miles south-west of Tokyo, Mount Fuji is Japan's most beloved symbol and its most distinctive geographic feature. This active volcano, which last erupted in 1707, is revered by the faithful, hiked up by climbers and painted by artists. 'Everyone adores Mount Fuji', exclaims the designer Keita Suzuki. Pairing this affection with Japan's national love of beer, Suzuki's *Fujiyama Glass* abstractly re-creates the famous mountain in drinking-glass form. An elegant cone of clear glass with a truncated point, it turns into a representation of Mount Fuji when filled with amber ale topped by a frothy white head.

The glass began life as Suzuki's submission to a design competition for new gifts from Japan. Mount Fuji's worldwide recognition made it a logical motif, but working out how to use it was another matter. 'I wanted to make something that didn't really exist yet', explains Suzuki. Although glasses for wine, martinis and champagne have prescribed shapes, in Japan the closest standard for beer is the tumblers used when large bottles are shared. Here was a need waiting to be met.

Although Suzuki's clever idea did not win the competition, it caught the attention of the judge, who recommended the glass for production. 'We don't usually do this sort of thing', says Yusuke Sugahara, whose family company has been producing its own hand-blown glassware since 1932. The in-house artisans thought the glass would be easy to make, but they changed their tune when the actual blowing began.

Producing the unusual shape is a feat of coordination, requiring the artisan to blow and spin the molten glass simultaneously, while inserting it into a wooden mould containing water that vaporizes when it comes into contact with the scorching glass. The trickiest part is blowing with force – it takes a lot to spread the glass all the way to the edge of the mould – without losing the steam. This steam prevents the glass and mould from touching, and is the key to the perfectly even exterior of the *Fujiyama Glass*.

The glasses are priced at Y3776 each (£29/$46), which may seem steep. But this sum – in yen, the same number as Mount Fuji's height in metres – is a small price to pay for such high levels of design quality and craftsmanship.

024

GUH
Gaku Otomo // Stagio
2006 // Iwatani Materials

In Japan, there is a right way and a wrong way to do just about everything, and throwing out the rubbish is no exception. Intent on reducing dumping, the country has for many years sorted its rubbish into burnable and non-burnable groups, but that's just the beginning. 'In the national drive to reduce waste and increase recycling, neighbourhoods, office buildings, towns and megalopolises are raising the number of trash categories – sometimes to dizzying heights', wrote the *New York Times* reporter Norimitsu Onishi in an article entitled 'How Do Japanese Dump Trash? Let Us Count the Myriad Ways' (May 2005).

Naturally, this boom has spawned many vessels for sorting and storing rubbish until its appointed pick-up day. Most are bulky, boxy affairs, and reside in the kitchen. But the product designer Gaku Otomo had another idea: 'Wouldn't it be good if you could divide trash right at your desk?' he reasoned. This would enable workers to separate their rubbish without leaving their seats and, better yet, would discourage the mixing of burnable and non-burnable refuse. To contrast with existing rectangular rubbish receptacles with two compartments, Otomo imagined a cylindrical bin. 'Round waste baskets have a long history', he explains. Yet finding a way to combine two tubes without sacrificing their geometric integrity required some study. Otomo's solution (reflected in the name *Guh*, 'hug' spelled backwards) was to create a tapered O-shaped bin and a second, C-shaped one to embrace it.

Angled forms add visual intrigue to the pieces, but also ease the injection-moulding manufacturing process. Produced in Japan by the plastics specialist Iwatani Materials in black, white or brown plastic, the twin bins both measure 37.5 cm (just under 1 ft 3 in.) in height but slant in opposite directions, and also vary in capacity: the C-bin holds 10.4 litres (just over 16 pints) and the O-bin 6.6 litres (10¾ pints). 'If the parts are too small, they are not easy to use,' says Otomo, 'but if they are too big they take up too much room.'

The two parts fit together perfectly, but can also enjoy their independence. While the 'O' is small enough to stand in the corner by itself, the 'C' can encircle a table leg, making the bins both space-saving and convenient.

025

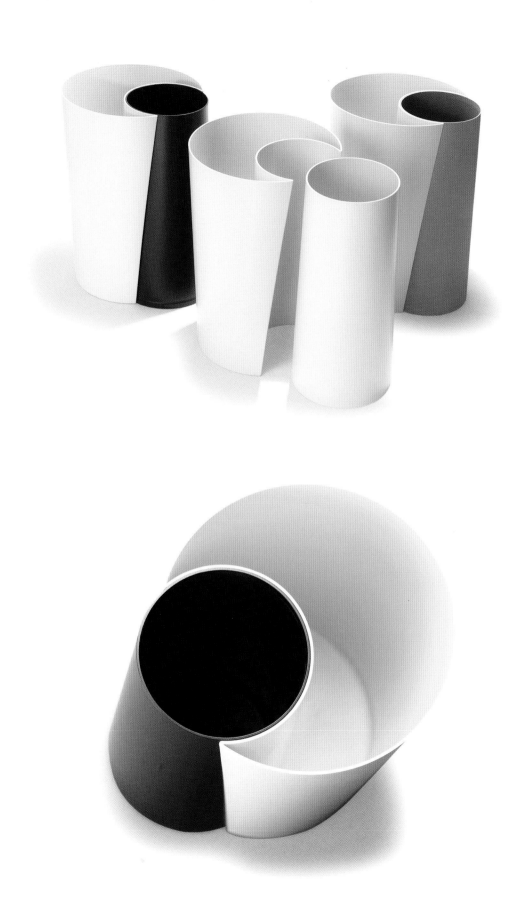

HANDS
Tonerico
2003 // Ceramic Japan

The polite way to offer something to someone in Japan – be it a business card or a bowl of rice – is with both hands. The *Hands*, a set of three nesting bowls in the form of cupped palms, embodies that gesture in white glazed porcelain. Designed by Yumi Masuko of the Tokyo-based design firm Tonerico, the bowls present food beautifully. And, by acknowledging the importance of the person on the receiving end, they do so with proper etiquette, too.

Tonerico, known for interiors that evoke traditional sensibilities and for products that carry a hidden meaning, was founded by Masuko, Hiroshi Yoneya and Ken Kimizuka. Although the team often designs together, Masuko took on the creation of the bowls without her partners. To realize her idea in high relief, she enlisted the aid of a ceramicist friend in Nagasaki who hand-sculpted the first prototypes from clay. Each of the three different sizes consisted of realistic, rounded fleshy fingers cupped closely together.

After the bowls' successful debut at the Milan Furniture Fair in 2003, the designers were keen to try their hands at mass production. The dish manufacturer Ceramic Japan agreed to make and, eventually, market the bowls. But in the process the shape evolved from a literal representation of hands to a more abstract one. The *Hands* is now made with plaster moulds, and the fingers are completely smoothed over on the outside and flattened on the inside.

Given the bowls' unique shape, they may not lend themselves easily to everyday dining. 'More than just a bowl, *Hands* conveys a message', explains Yoneya. Although functionality was only one of several design considerations, people continue to buy the bowls in part because they work well. Between what Tonerico terms the 'family' of sizes – father, mother and child – the bowls can comfortably hold anything from an entire salad to a single piece of fruit. And customers report that the notches at the tip of the thumbs are the perfect place on which to rest the communal chopsticks used for serving. 'We are learning from our users too', says Yoneya, smiling.

026

HANGER TREE
Un-do Design
2011

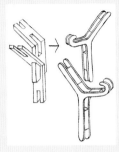

Composed of wooden hangers that slot inside one another to make up a stand, Un-do Design's *Hanger Tree* is a playful solution to the problem of clothing clutter that plagues many Japanese homes and apartments. The lack of wardrobe space means that clothing tends to get hung on every available protuberance: wall hooks, window frames and doorknobs are all fair game. 'I hang my clothing wherever I possibly can', says Un-do Design partner Rui Matsuo. Adaptable to rooms of different sizes and clothing of various types, the *Hanger Tree* helps to keep things tidy and amuses its owner at the same time.

A design duo comprised of Matsuo and Yasutaka Kimura, Un-do Design is well acquainted with ways to suspend clothes. In addition to elaborate display structures for fashion brands, the company had already designed a folding wooden hanger, and the freestanding *Hanger Tree* is an outgrowth of those products.

Each *Hanger Tree* comes as a kit of twelve individual wooden pieces that the owner assembles at home. In common with their conventional wire counterparts, the hangers are able to wear jackets and other clothes on their broad shoulders. But that is not their *raison d'être*; instead, they are arranged vertically into a stand – the exact arrangement is the owner's choice – and the garments perch on their curved hooks and splayed tips that jut out every which way. 'Our first idea was to design one product that can change shapes', explains Matsuo.

What makes this possible is the unique joining system holding the stand together: the hangers are unusually thick, measuring 3.8 cm (1½ in.) in depth, but are not solid; in each hanger, openings at either end and where the three 'limbs' meet enable it to intersect with other hangers. With the ease of assembling toy blocks, the stand's components slide into place.

Fabricated by Kimura in his off-hours at the furniture factory where he earns his living, the hangers are made from wood cut during forest thinning. Each one consists of two layers of plywood, with birch blocks in between. Aided by Matsuo, he glues the wood together, sands the rough edges and finishes each one with a protective oil coating.

027

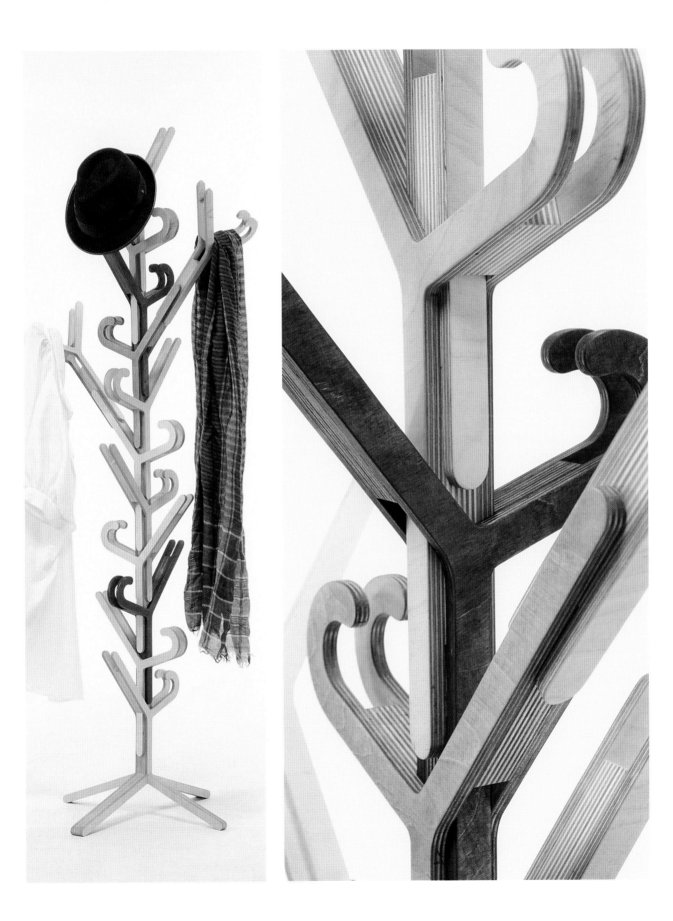

HIGASHIYA MONAKA
Shinichiro Ogata // Simplicity
2003

Traditional sweets known as *wagashi* have been savoured in Japan for centuries. Comprising different ingredients, such as azuki bean paste and chestnut or rice flour, and made in various shapes, the many types of *wagashi* are exquisitely crafted by skilled confectioners into edible works of art, and, accompanied by green tea, they are still the preferred sweet for formal occasions. By contrast, when it comes to impromptu get-togethers or casual parties, Western-style chocolates and biscuits are the norm. Convinced that he could update *wagashi*'s stodgy character without compromising their rich history, Shinichiro Ogata decided to marry his design talents with those of a traditional sweets specialist.

A designer with a broad range of experience and interests, Ogata has built his practice on the renewal of Japanese heritage. Working in many media, including ceramics, metals, lacquerware and wood, Ogata collaborates with craftspeople around the country. His goal is not simply to keep the country's endangered arts alive but also, more importantly, to revitalize and integrate them into the contemporary Japanese lifestyle. *Wagashi*, which had been unchanged for hundreds of years, were ripe for reinvention. 'I wanted to change the way we use *wagashi*', explains Ogata. So he created his own brand, called Higashi ('daily sweets'), covering treats ranging from spherical balls of azuki bean paste to slender, stick-like 'sandwich' biscuits. The latter, an elegant remake of the jam-filled wafers known as *monaka*, contrast sharply with the usual circular or rectangular forms. 'I wanted the minimum width and the maximum length', says the designer, but his collaborator would not countenance this idea at first. 'Japan's craftsmen have wonderful techniques but they shy away from challenges', says Ogata, but gentle persuasion convinced the confectioner to give it a go.

The rice-flour wafers are cooked in a circular steel mould with spoke-like slots, and come in three different colours – white, tan or black – depending on the cooking time, or on whether bamboo charcoal was added to the batter (this has no taste at all, and is added purely for its colour). The trough-shaped biscuits come with separate sachets of fillings: azuki bean jam, puréed purple sweet potato or, Ogata's personal favourite, black sesame paste. The components are packaged at the brand's factory in Tokyo into colour-coordinated boxes resembling Western-style chocolate bars, but final assembly of the biscuits is left to the consumer, so that the wafers remain dry and crisp until the last moment.

028

HIROSHIMA ARM CHAIR
Naoto Fukasawa
2008 // Maruni Wood Industry

'I always wanted to design a chair made of nice wood', says Naoto Fukasawa. When he began collaborating with furniture manufacturer Maruni Wood Industry, he soon got his wish. The *Hiroshima Arm Chair*, named after the company's home town, is beautifully proportioned, lightweight and exquisitely crafted. As importantly, the chair back and connected armrests offer excellent support for the upper back from just about any sitting position, and by supporting the upper back, the chair relieves pressure on the lower back.

While Fukasawa brought his high aesthetic standards and design expertise to the table, Maruni contributed decades of manufacturing experience and technical know-how. Founded in 1928, the company prides itself on integrating industrial manufacturing methods with Japan's traditional craftsmanship sensibility. Although the advanced techniques used by Maruni's skilled labourers rely on machines, the furniture-makers wield their electric saws and sanders with craftsworkers' critical eyes and meticulous attention to detail – exemplifying the concept of *monozukuri,* or the reverence for 'making things', that is still prevalent in Japan today.

While Fukasawa was armed with an awareness of the seat angles needed to buttress the body, his best design guide was his empirical understanding of what makes a comfortable chair. 'People do not usually sit facing straight forward', he explains. 'A lazy style of sitting, leaning in one direction, is more natural.' With that in mind, he rounded the back of the chair and attached it to the arms, creating the sensation that the body is being 'held'. But arriving at this solution required much fine-tuning and repeated testing for back support and structural stability. 'We could not have reached this quality product without the experience of Maruni's master engineers', says Fukasawa.

The first chairs in the series to come on the market were made of beech or oak, lightly finished with urethane or oil. The back, arms, legs and seat are constructed individually but fit together seamlessly, as if carved from a single block of wood. As Fukasawa states, 'In the past, it was not possible to achieve this smoothness with mass production.' But the traditional method of allowing nature to age the wood over time will bring out the chair's true beauty.

029

HK GRAVITY PEARLS
Nosigner
2010 // Japan Imitation Pearl & Glass Articles Association

For Nosigner, design is not a process of creation but rather one of discovery. Instead of inventing new forms, the firm researches the relationships between people and their surroundings. Its findings are akin to site constraints facing an architect, and inform the design decisions that guide the company towards logical solutions – be it for an entire interior, a solo chair or even a single magnetic pearl.

Although jewellery-makers often engage the services of experienced designers, it is another matter with makers of artificial pearls. After years of supplying other companies, a consortium of Japan's foremost manufacturers of synthetic pearls was keen to develop a jewellery brand of its own. Lacking its own design capability, it looked to Nosigner. 'At first I refused their offer', says Eisuke Tachikawa, a representative of the design firm. Nosigner reasoned that its client's expertise lay in the making of a jewellery component, not in the creation of jewellery itself; 'They do not know the rules of the market', Tachikawa explains. Instead, the designers counter-proposed with an offer to develop a new material. Yet in the end, that collaboration yielded not only a material but also, with the addition of a little creativity from the wearer, a finished product.

Incorporating its client's manufacturing technique, developed more than a hundred years ago, Nosigner created a cluster of imitation pearls that the wearer can form and re-form into a bracelet, necklace, earrings or ring. No string links the luminous balls, which seem to stick together magically; their connectivity is the work of magnets concealed inside. 'We did not design the [pearls'] shape – it is just a round ball,' states Tachikawa, 'but we realized a new relationship between technique and market.'

As if acknowledging the pearls' man-made origins, Nosigner bottled each set in a test tube capped with a cork. Made by a scientific-glass supplier, the tubes are etched with the brand logo, HK. The name is a play on words: it is pronounced 'haku', a Japanese word that means 'white' (a reference to the pearls' milky colour), but the logo's stylized Roman letters are abstracted from the Japanese character read as 'izumi', the name of the artificial-pearl industry's home town.

030

HONEY-COMB MESH + BRACELET
Masako Ban // Acrylic
2007

A square polyester-mesh bag coupled with a circular acrylic handle, the *Honey-comb Mesh + Bracelet* epitomizes Masako Ban's industrial aesthetic. Ban, an accessories designer with a passion for synthetic materials, transforms sponge, rubber, aluminium, mosquito screening and other ready-made products into bold jewellery and beautiful handbags – each one an elegant fashion statement with an element of surprise.

Ban's awareness of materials began when she worked briefly for her husband, the architect Shigeru Ban, who is best known for his buildings constructed from paper and cardboard tubing. She went on to become a self-taught graphic designer, but making acrylic jewellery was her true calling and she teamed up with an architectural model-maker able to craft chokers, rings and bracelets from the translucent material. 'I always design what I want for myself', she says.

Handbags were a natural segue for Ban. Together with her younger sister, a costume designer with a sewing machine, Ban creates prototype satchels, clutches and eco-bags from heavy-duty materials intended for wall coverings, upholstery and industrial use. 'Japan makes excellent textiles, but famous designers rarely use them', she states. Ban came across the polyester mesh at a textiles fair in Tokyo. Used mostly for protective clothing that shields outdoor workers from bee stings and airborne detritus, the thick but airy material consists of two layers of honeycomb netting connected by thin fibres. It is produced in a small factory in rural Toyama Prefecture, where the need for strong outerwear is great. 'I like to support local companies', explains Ban; she also works with Tokyo suppliers, such as the manufacturer of buttons and buckles that makes her signature acrylic handles, and the handbag-maker that turns her unusual materials into bags that she sells at her shop, Acrylic, in central Tokyo.

Flaunting its functional fabric, the bag consists of a mesh exterior, a durable nylon interior and an acrylic handle worn on the wrist in the manner of a bangle. A concealed magnetic snap completes the bag without compromising its geometric purity.

031

HONEYCOMB LAMP
Kouichi Okamoto // Kyouei Design
2006

In its flat cardboard-box packaging, the *Honeycomb Lamp* is simply an unassuming block of paper. But when its filmy layers are unfolded, its purpose is revealed as it magically turns into a freestanding fixture with the curvaceous figure of an iconic Western lamp, shade included. Made entirely from a type of light traditional paper known as *denguri*, the lamp is the product of Kouichi Okamoto of Kyouei Design.

When designing, instead of starting from scratch, Okamoto frequently begins with an existing object and transforms it into something completely new (see also *Reconstruction Chandelier*, page 154). This process has fascinated Okamoto since childhood, when he lived near a factory that manufactured plastic model kits. Guided only by his imagination, Okamoto used the factory's discarded bits and pieces to build robots and other toys of his own invention.

Okamoto has not lost that playful spirit, and even now, as an adult, he appreciates children's pop-up books with their 3D illustrations – the structure that inspired the *Honeycomb Lamp*. 'I thought the various pages could wrap around a light bulb and become the lampshade', explains the designer. He soon realized, however, that this technique limited him to a 180-degree enclosure. To make a full circle, he needed another model, and so he turned to *denguri* paper instead.

A speciality of the island of Shikoku, *denguri* consists of thin sheets of machine-made *washi* paper (a traditional Japanese paper) glued together along one edge to form a rigid spine for a 3D shape. Once dyed and cut, the paper wads typically become ornaments for Japan's many festivals. *Denguri* is normally made in twenty-layered reams, and the manufacturer initially rejected Okamoto's request for a 240-sheet wad; but, eventually, he relented.

The wet paper is assembled into a pile about 2 cm (¾ in.) thick, and is then dried for about two days, depending on the season and the climate. After that, the lamp's profile is incised at the factory with a mould resembling an oversized pastry cutter. The lamp is formed by pinning the two end sheets together, which pops the paper layers open in a honeycomb pattern. The opening at the bottom accommodates the electric cord; the one at the top throws light upwards. When seen from the side, the 45-cm-tall (about 17¾ in.) lamp completely conceals its 10-watt bulb (the wattage had to be low to avoid the risk of the paper burning), but even this strength fills the entire object with a soft glow.

032

HUMIDIFIER
Naoto Fukasawa
2003 // Plus Minus Zero

In Japan, where the winter air is dry, the humidifier is a popular and often necessary appliance. Unsurprisingly, a multitude of air-moisturizing devices are available. Although most are nondescript affairs programmed simply to get the job done, and are put away when temperatures start to rise again, Naoto Fukasawa's version is also a sculptural object that is beautiful to look at all year round.

Fukasawa's humidifier was made for the housewares brand Plus Minus Zero, which the designer helped to establish in 2003 (see also *Toaster*, page 200). In the hope that clever, well-designed goods make daily life more enjoyable, the company aims to improve on standard solutions – including humidifiers. Although there was no need to better the appliance's simple mechanism, there was plenty of scope for fixing its form.

This designer humidifier works in the same way as any other – its sole function is to heat water until it turns to steam – but outwardly gives no hint of its role; in fact, with its puffy, 30-cm-diameter (11¾ in.) plastic doughnut shape, it hardly resembles an appliance at all. 'I thought the shape should be strange', says Fukasawa. 'I wanted customers to ask "What is this?" when they see it.' Bursts of steam emitted by a sunken opening in the centre suggest the object's purpose, but the switch and plug are tucked under the base and do not detract from its perfect roundness.

Although it appears to be a single smooth volume, Fukasawa's humidifier consists of two parts. The bottom part, which contains the electrical apparatus, is completely covered by the bigger top, where the water tank is stored. Because of its injection-moulding manufacture, this top shell had to be made in two pieces. But ultrasonic bonding, painting and buff-polishing erase the seam entirely. 'It's the same process as for a motorbike helmet', explains Fukasawa.

In keeping with Plus Minus Zero's credo, the humidifier comes in a wide array of cheery colours, ranging from the perennially popular white to a bold red and a deep blue, so that there is a hue to match any interior.

033

INFOBAR A01
Naoto Fukasawa
2011 // KDDI/iida

Naoto Fukasawa's *Infobar A01* is a smartphone with attitude. With its contrasting colours, the snappy plastic case demands attention; the vertically scrolling interface, which consists of widgets that slide around in the manner of game pieces, challenges that of competitors; and, lined up assertively across the bottom, a band of three tile-shaped keys – 'menu', 'home' and 'back' – takes commands with a tap of a finger. Yet the phone's streamlined shape fits the palm or pocket so comfortably that it almost feels like an extension of the body. Unsurprisingly, that was one of Fukasawa's intentions when he launched the first *Infobar* in 2003.

Unlike the clamshell-style mobile phones that flooded the market at that time, Fukasawa's appliance felt good to hold. Its elegant bar shape sat comfortably in the hand, and its square, tile-like keys seemed to anticipate the finger's natural action. The next generation, a lozenge-shaped device with state-of-the-art technology, came four years later. Fully expecting the then-simple mobile phone to expand into an internet-friendly, information-dispensing device,

Fukasawa aptly named the entire series *Infobar*. And from that idea, the *A01* was practically inevitable.

A smooth segue from its predecessors, the *A01* deftly adapted the Infobar's salient features to the Android smartphone format used by mobile-phone giant KDDI's iida brand (see also *X-Ray*, page 218). The widgets and icons, which appear as a collage of small tinted rectangles (created in collaboration with the web and interface designer Yugo Nakamura), are reminiscent of the tiled keypad of the earlier Infobars.

Picking up where the *Infobar 2* left off, the *A01* makes a signature feature of its bold colour schemes. Among the five different combinations are the tri-toned Nishikigoi (named after a type of red-and-white carp) and the delectable Chocopink (two shades of candy-coloured rose coupled with rich cocoa-brown). While the need to accommodate the smartphone's screen resulted in a widening of the sleek *Infobar* silhouette, bevelled edges and rounded corners soften the shape so that the phone naturally belongs close at hand.

034

ISHIKORO
Masaru Suzuki // Ottaipinu
2006 // Yoshii Towel Company

Bathing as a form of relaxation is steeped in history in Japan, and has been enjoyed for centuries by people throughout the archipelago. But today most of the population does not have the pleasure of luxuriating at home in a deep cedar tub with a garden view. The vast majority of people must settle for a watered-down version: soaping in the shower and then soaking in a tub made of enamelled metal or moulded plastic. Determined to improve life for his fellow bathers, the textile designer Masaru Suzuki teamed up with manufacturer Yoshii Towel Company to create a series of bath mats that evoke nature – even in the middle of the city.

One of 160 towel-makers located in Imabari, a town of 115,000 inhabitants on the island of Shikoku, Yoshii is known for its exceptionally soft towels. But Suzuki had another idea in mind: 'I wanted to make a towel textured like grass and a bath mat with the feel of pebbles', he explains. Persuaded by Suzuki's pitch (he had brought a sample of live grass to make his point), the manufacturer decided to give it a go. But realizing Suzuki's vision proved to be no small undertaking. In order to achieve sufficient roughness, the 'grass' towel required a customized yarn composed of cotton thread and strands of hemp. For the *Ishikoro* bath mat (opposite, top), named after the Japanese for 'pebbles', developing a prototype from Suzuki's sketches took a year. The irregular outlines of the 'stones', made by tracing the outlines of river rocks, were easy for Yoshii's sophisticated looms to handle, but re-creating the real stones' volume and depth with cotton thread was a lengthy process that required the addition of more and more loopy piles.

Nearly 1 cm (⅜ in.) thick, the *Ishikoro* mat has considerably more depth than the usual terry-cloth floor covering, and its pronounced pattern not only resembles stones but also gently suggests the sensation of stepping on them. 'Walking barefoot on rocks by a river is very good for the health of the feet and muscles', comments Suzuki. Other models in his range of bath mats include the *Chikurin* mat, which resembles bamboo stalks (opposite, bottom), and the *Suna* mat, laced with polyester threads and recalling raked sand.

035

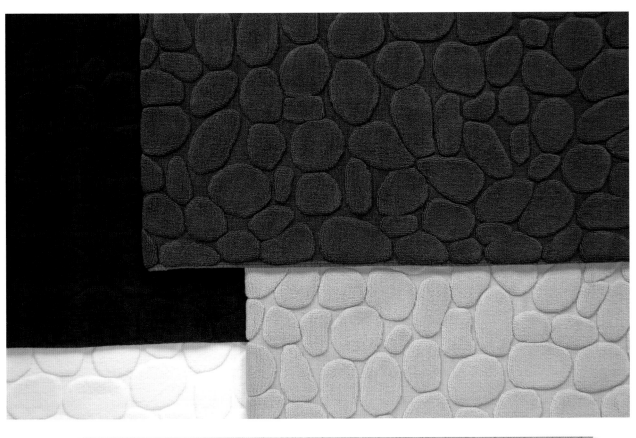

KADOKESHI
Hideo Kanbara // Barakan Design
2003 // Kokuyo

As every artist, primary-school pupil or other pencil user knows, an eraser's best feature is its corners: they can obliterate even tiny errors as no other part of the eraser can. Capitalizing on this trait, Hideo Kanbara's *Kadokeshi* is practically all corners. Unlike the usual small rectangular piece of rubber, the *Kadokeshi* is a string of staggered cubes; when one pointy tip wears down, another one is just around the corner.

Named with a combination of Japanese words meaning 'corner' and 'rub out', the *Kadokeshi* began as a submission to a competition for new product ideas hosted by the Kokuyo stationery company. At the time Kanbara was busily creating plumbing fixtures as an in-house designer for Toto, a manufacturer of plumbing products, but he thought he would give desk goods a try.

Kanbara reasoned that the competition would draw hundreds of entries, so he knew that he had to come up with something eye-catching. Overlooked by designers, erasers were the perfect medium. For inspiration, the designer did not have to look any further than his own memory bank. 'I remembered borrowing an eraser from the girl at the next desk when I was eight years old', he reminisces. 'She got angry at me for using the fresh corners.'

At first Kanbara investigated sharp-edged shapes, such as stars, and he even considered making a many-cornered eraser roll that shopkeepers could cut for customers on request. In the end, he opted for the block of cubes. 'I still wanted it to be recognizably an eraser', he explains, but, as the 5-cm-long (2 in.) *Kadokeshi* is composed of a series of cubes measuring 1 cm (⅜ in.), it can double as a small ruler. The cubes are arranged in two layers, and on each layer they are set corner-to-corner in the manner of a chequerboard. To shore up the connections, Kanbara thickened the points of contact by rounding out the inner corners.

Being able to break off cubes might be seen as a desirable feature, but the manufacturer used a stronger plastic material than is usual, in order to keep the eraser intact. Despite the *Kadokeshi*'s complexity, its unique form was easy to make with an injection-moulding process. While it ranked in the competition's lowest prize category, the eraser was first among all the winners to go into production.

036

KAI TABLE
Naoki Hirakoso // Hirakoso Design
2002

At first glance, the *Kai Table* is simply a smooth, square slab of wood set on the floor. But a few quick moves result in its parts unfolding, sliding and lifting to reveal phenomenal storage capabilities: twelve differently configured compartments accessed from all directions. The table, designed by Naoki Hirakoso in collaboration with Takamitsu Kitahara, was inspired by traditional puzzle boxes, the drawers and moving panels of which must be opened in sequence, and it conceals the perfect places to store the overflow and messiness of daily life. Its name is apt, *kai* being an obscure Japanese character that appears most often as part of a phrase meaning 'versatile' or 'open to possibilities'.

The storage consists of various receptacles that range in size and shape from small drawers that glide out from the side to large bins opened from above, all the better to accommodate pens, newspapers, remote-controls and other objects that normally clutter up Japan's typically tiny living rooms. By hiding all these objects from view, the 90-cm-square (35½ in.) table tidies up the entire space. But when all its cabinetry is closed, the divided wooden box acts as a table that is low enough for floor-cushion seating and high enough to partner Japanese sofas or chairs, which tend to be lower than their Western counterparts. Successful assembly depends on the perfect alignment of all the table's parts. The most challenging of these are the invisible hinges of the top flaps: once they have been put in place, adjustment is out of the question. 'The screws have to be positioned very, very carefully', explains Hirakoso.

The *Kai Table* was initially fabricated by a carpenter on the island of Kyushu, where Hirakoso worked as chief display designer for the Conran Shop in Fukuoka City, but it is now constructed by furniture-maker Minerva. The table is made of plywood, and is clad with a veneer of blond shina-wood (shina is a member of the lime family). 'Whatever you can see is covered with shina', says the designer.

A single sheet of wood blankets the entire top. Although it has been cut to create the various flaps, it quietly unites the surface with its unbroken grain. But beneath that uniform cover is a place for just about any object its owner wishes to put away.

037

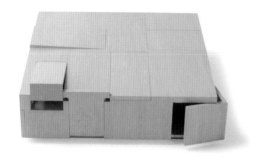
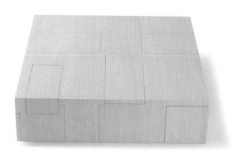

KAMIKIRIMUSHI
Satoshi Nakagawa // Tripod Design
2006 // Harac

Named after the Japanese word for the Asian long-horned beetle but resembling a computer mouse, Tripod Design's *Kamikirimushi* is a cutting instrument with universal appeal. Intended for users of all ages and abilities, it is modelled on the iconic computer accessory, and with a simple drag and click makes the act of slicing paper as easy as surfing the net.

As do all Tripod Design projects (see also *Chibion Touch*, page 58), this one began with field research, in this case in children's nurseries and elderly-care centres. 'We have been focusing on the average person,' says the firm's founder, Satoshi Nakagawa, 'but what does "average" really mean?' Keen to find out, Nakagawa and his team learned that ordinary shears are difficult for many to manage. In addition to standard scissors being problematic for left-handed people, some children and elderly people do not have the strength to hold scissors in the air while cutting or opening and closing the blades. But many of those unable to manipulate scissors can still slide a mouse around with ease.

Although the *Kamikirimushi* was neither the firm's first pair of scissors nor its first computer mouse, it was its first product to combine the function of one with the form of the other. Smaller than the typical mouse but easier to grip, the cutter has a plastic body, from which projects a small appendage that holds a rotating ceramic blade of the sort normally used by factories to slice thin strips of filmy materials; pressing lightly on this tip enables the blade to slice through paper. (The tip brings to mind the horns of the giant beetles that many Japanese children keep as pets, a fact that explains the cutter's name.) While the tabletop provides the necessary resistance, the cutter glides around, cutting even complex curves without ever nicking the skin.

Manufactured in Japan by metal-goods producer Harac, the cutter was a runaway success. 'I think that good design should be universal', says Nakagawa; equally popular among professional graphic designers as with denizens of day-care centres, the *Kamikirimushi* proves that it can be.

038

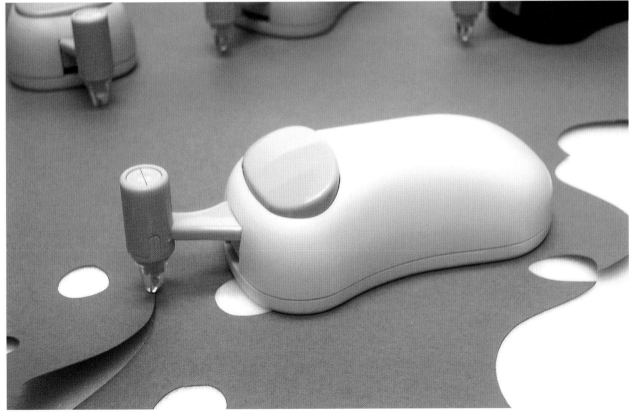

KIBISO SANDALS
Reiko Sudo // Nuno
2011

These flip-flops made of waste silk combine two of Japan's fading traditions. Sericulture (silkworm rearing and silk production) was once a thriving industry, but today only two silk mills remain. And craftsworkers who hand-weave *waraji* shoes – straw footwear once worn by the masses but now made mostly by special order for kabuki actors and Buddhist monks – are dwindling. By binding the dyeing technique and discarded silk by-product in her *Kibiso Sandals*, textile designer Reiko Sudo gives both a new lease of life.

Sudo's shoe project began with a trek to the Tsuruoka silk centre in northern Japan. 'When I went there, I found this coarse material and immediately fell in love with it', she says. Kibiso fibres, which are spewed out by silkworms, coat the raw silk threads as well as the cocoon itself, and are removed during processing. Yet for Sudo, who frequently incorporates such unexpected materials as feathers and stainless-steel threads into her fabrics (see also *Tiggy*, page 196), the sinuous strings were full of potential. Untreated, they were not only visually interesting but also laden with healing properties. Containing a moisture-rich protein called sericin, kibiso acts as a

natural moisturizer and also blocks the sun's ultraviolet rays. 'It protects the caterpillar inside the cocoon from sunlight', explains Sudo. Although the cosmetics industry has been capitalizing on these qualities for years by adding pulverized kibiso to skincare products, the grass-like strands had been overlooked for other uses.

Kibiso strands are similar to straw, and Sudo thought they would be the perfect medium for Tsuruoka's traditional weavers, who, like their ancestors, still grow and harvest special rice stalks and weave them into floor cushions, backpacks, beds for cats and, in the case of one lone craftsman, *waraji* sandals. Adapting his technique for use with kibiso was a natural step.

Because of its flexibility and lightness, plastic string forms the warp, or inner structure, of the *Kibiso Sandals*, but it is completely concealed by the kibiso weft; it takes about 100 silkworm cocoons to produce one pair of oval-soled shoes topped with matching braided straps. Conforming to the sole of the foot as it bends, the sandals are suitable for indoor use but might wear thin after a few months of pounding the Tokyo pavement.

039

KINOISHI
Taku Satoh // Taku Satoh Design Office
2010 // Kijiya

Kinoishi – facsimiles of river stones amazingly realistically rendered in wood – are lovely to look at but even better to hold. As if it were worn by years of exposure to water and wind, each irregularly shaped but rounded piece fits the palm of the hand so comfortably that it is hard to put down. Although it was invented as a toy for children, this set of twenty 'stones made of wood' (*ki no ishi* in Japanese) created by the designer Taku Satoh is irresistible to people of all ages.

The project actually began with a stool. Satoh had been one of several designers invited by the Japan Design Committee to collaborate with makers of wooden furniture in Hida Takayama, a densely forested region in Gifu Prefecture. Under the aegis of the committee's 'Furniture for a Personal Use' project, he created a sculptural seat for putting on shoes, perfectly sized for the Japanese home's typically tight entrance hall. Named *Kamachi* after the built-in step that separates the differing floor levels between the entrance and living areas, the curvaceous stool looks especially beautiful when not in use.

Unlike many designers matched with local craftspeople, Satoh was keen to continue the collaboration after the *Kamachi* entered production. But this time he approached the creation of the product from a different direction. 'Unlike with the stool, I did not design the shapes [of the stones]', says the designer. 'I received these shapes from nature.'

Yet Satoh did choose the stones on which the wood blocks are modelled – an important design decision in disguise. He is an avid surfer, and collects rocks from the various beaches and riverbeds he has known and loved. Instead of making drawings of the selected stones, his staff took 3D photographs of them and then converted the images into computer data. Using this digital information as their guide, the woodworkers turned pieces of waste wood into 'pretend' stones that can generate hours of play.

'Today kids just play on their computers', laments Satoh. 'They do not go to the park or play outside.' The *Kinoishi* sends an important message, and its abstract shapes actively stimulate the imagination; they can be rocks, blocks or anything a child wants them to be.

040

KNOT
Shigeki Fujishiro // Shigeki Fujishiro Design
2009

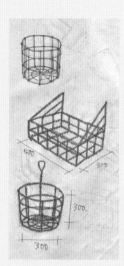

Metre upon metre of chunky red rope looped and tied together equals a universal storage basket that is suitable for use on land or at sea. Appropriately titled *Knot*, the basket was designed by Shigeki Fujishiro at his studio in a former school in Tokyo's Setagaya Ward. Although he is formally trained in space design, Fujishiro earns his living creating functional objects with his own two hands. 'If I make something by myself, people can feel my energy', he explains.

A lot of energy has gone into the making of the *Knot*. Fujishiro's inspiration came from an image of a wall-mounted storage basket he had seen in a book, but he had to teach himself nautical knotting and splicing techniques before he could begin to realize his version. He also had to find a suitable material, one that would be stiff enough to hold a shape yet pliable enough for tying. Fortunately, he found the solution at a local net-making company. The firm, which produces safety and screening devices

for playgrounds and athletics fields, offered polyester ropes in a wide range of colours. Although yellow is Fujishiro's favourite, he selected red for its fresh, fashionable image. Using samples sent by the company, he began making models both big and small.

Initially Fujishiro had envisioned a hanging basket, but the rigidity of the rope opened up other possibilities. 'It was so stiff, it could stand by itself', he says. Measuring 1 cm (⅜ in.) in diameter, the rope was too thick for purely knotted connections. Fortunately, though, it melted easily, and this enabled Fujishiro to loop, splice, tie and fuse the braids into a rounded square basket defined by a uniform grid of red rope.

While the basket initially attracted attention from an overseas buyer who featured it in his Los Angeles shop, the *Knot* quickly caught on in Japan as well. 'In Japan, there are many ropes at shrines and other spiritual places', reflects Fujishiro. 'Maybe we feel that rope is a special thing.'

041

KUDAMEMO
D-Bros // Draft
2009

In Japan, where gift-giving is a deeply entrenched social ritual, the fruit gift box can approach an art form. These beautiful assemblies of perfectly shaped produce are such a feast for the eye that it seems a shame to eat their contents. The *Kudamemo* resolves that conundrum. This clever product (in fact there are two, one modelled on a red Fuji apple and the other on a green Anjou pear) combines the good looks of fresh fruit with the function of a notepad. It sports an equally clever moniker: its name is a play on words, merging *kudamono*, the Japanese word for 'fruit', with the English word 'memo'.

The *Kudamemo* was created by D-Bros, the product-design division of the advertising agency Draft. 'Our mission is to create 3D objects conceived by graphic designers', states Masashi Tentaku of D-Bros. Many of the group's products utilize paper and printing technology, but it was bookbinding that inspired the *Kudamemo*.

Instead of beginning with the goal of creating a particular product, D-Bros started with an existing form: the book. By opening a book 360 degrees so that its front and back covers touched, it turned a flat object into a freestanding one. 'I pondered how we could use this shape and what we could make with it', says Tentaku. Rounded like a cylinder, this newly found form lent itself naturally to a pad of paper with removable sheets.

The team considered different profiles for the pages, eventually settling on fruit forms that sit comfortably in the hand and look good on a desktop. Each *Kudamemo* consists of 150 off-white pages rimmed with red or green ink and accented with a brown seed printed near its core.

A Tokyo-based press handles the offset printing, and each *Kudamemo* is assembled by hand at a small factory in neighbouring Saitama Prefecture. As in the case of a book, the pages are glued and then bound with cloth tape – a labour-intensive task that yields perfect pear- or apple-shaped alignment; they are then topped with a wooden stem. Finally, a paper clip holds the first and last pages together, concealing the core. 'Because of the clip, *Kudamemo* holds its shape even if only half its pages are left', explains Tentaku.

042

KULMS CHAIR
MisoSoupDesign
2009 // Lerival

The *Kulms Chair 02*, a curvy plane supported by a pair of triangulated legs, is as much at home in a tiny New York studio as in a Japanese '1 LDK' apartment (one bedroom, with living, dining and kitchen areas). Having lived in both cities, the designers of the chair, architects Daisuke Nagatomo and Minnie Jan of MisoSoupDesign, should know. In common with its predecessor, the uniquely shaped *Kulms Chair 01*, the *02* is hardly petite, but several can be stacked neatly in one space-saving pile.

Inspired by an image of a bamboo stalk, the architects borrowed the botanical word 'culm' (the stem of a plant) for their chair's name. But the physical form of the seat emerged after the two began fiddling with some small paper Post-it notes, cutting a bit here, taping a bit there. 'Basically, we wondered what type of stacking chair we could make with one piece of paper', explains Nagatomo. They settled on the *01*'s tripod-like form, with one single centrally placed triangulated leg at the back of the chair (see page 24, centre of row 9), because they liked the fact that the chair looked as if it were floating.

The designers were not content to take a back seat during the production phase and started approaching furniture-making factories directly, but ended up engaging New York-based furniture-design company Lerival to liaise with the manufacturer and market the finished *Kulms Chair 01*. 'Lerival works with architects all the time, so it understood where we were coming from and respected our ideas', explains Jan.

The architects' dream was to make the *01* chair from a single sheet of bent plywood that would mimic their paper prototype, but after the fabricator baulked at this the chair was built from cross-sectional slices instead. Guided by the architects' digital drawings, a computerized milling machine cut the required twenty-four strips from a sheet of plywood just under 2 cm (¾ in.) thick – a very precise and efficient method that minimized post-production waste. Glue and headless nails hold the layers together, but this construction is completely disguised by the finished *01*'s black lacquer paint.

Beautiful as well as functional, the *Kulms Chair 01* was ideal for residential customers. But concerns about its stability led to the production of the *Kulms Chair 02*, which has two hind legs and is targeted at commercial venues, such as hotels and cafes. Although not as daring as its predecessor, the *Kulms Chair 02* is still a dramatic departure from the usual restaurant fare.

043

LUCANO
Chiaki Murata // Metaphys
2009 // Hasegawa Kogyo

The notion of a ladder with eye appeal may seem unlikely, but the *Lucano* dispels that doubt in an instant. Elegantly proportioned and simply appointed, this small stepladder can help people to reach a high shelf safely, but is attractive enough not to need stowing away after use. Those qualities were precisely the goal of its designer, Chiaki Muratata, the founder of Osaka-based design firm Metaphys.

Murata teams up regularly with local manufacturers to work on new and improved versions of their products, be it a folding toothbrush, a vacuum cleaner or a bento lunch box. When Hasegawa Kogyo, Japan's leading producer of ladders, invited him to collaborate on revamping the cumbersome and visually lacking stepladder, Murata gladly stepped up to the challenge.

In common with all Hasegawa Kogyo's products, the *Lucano* is made of extruded aluminium (a lightweight material that is capable of bearing heavy loads), but the similarity ends there. In an effort to tidy up the typical ladder's look, Murata started by modifying its construction. Retooling the legs and treads with a triangular section yielded a slimmer and cleaner appearance. The various components slide neatly into place, invisibly fastened with hidden screws – a rung up from the bolts and hardware that mar the appearance of most conventional climbing devices. The whole is then unified by a coating of matt black or white paint, or Metaphys's signature shade of orange.

Stylish enough for a fashionable boutique, the *Lucano* is equally at home in the typically small Japanese dwelling. With living area so limited, people in Japan are skilled at using whatever space they have. Any empty nook or cranny is a potential storage space, even if it is quite high up. Yet despite stepladders' utility in accessing out-of-the-way places, they are rarely used. 'Most stepladders are hidden away and difficult to take out, so people tend to stand on chairs instead', explains Murata.

When its legs are collapsed, the *Lucano* ladder bears a slight resemblance to an insect with folded wings, hence its name, the Spanish word for 'stag beetle'. But whether closed or open, this beautiful ladder ought to be seen as well as used.

044

MANY HEELS
Itaru Yonenaga // No Control Air
2005

A knitted scarf made from a continuous string of socks, the *Many Heels* makes a strong fashion statement but in an architectural way. This unusual neck-warmer is the product of No Control Air, a husband-and-wife clothing company in Osaka that has put the iconic sock shape to an entirely unexpected and unprecedented use.

The inception of the *Many Heels* was as much a process of discovery as one of design, and was sparked after No Control Air's Itaru Yonenaga visited a knitwear factory, where he spied a long woolly tube among the various samples strewn about the floor. Trained as an architect, he was captivated by the pure form: a length of L-shaped units arranged ankle-band-to-toe and accented by rounded heel caps in between. 'Most fashion designers would have seen a chain of socks, but I saw a muffler', says Yonenaga. By disassociating the woolly tube from the sock's mundane purpose of covering the foot, Yonenaga hit upon a new way to use its existing shape.

Once stripped of its meaning, the sock form took on a new life. 'The heel of a sock is very cute', reasoned Yonenaga. The gently rounded corner is usually hidden inside a shoe, where its decorative quality is lost. 'I thought it would be interesting to show it', says the designer.

Although he knew that putting socks, even brand-new ones, near the face might be frowned upon in Japan, Yonenaga commissioned the factory to make sock-shaped scarves on its high-tech knitting machine. 'It's a very simple system', he states. 'If I pay money, the factory will make it.' No complicated contracts or commitments for large orders were needed.

In common with all No Control Air products, the *Many Heels* is intended for use by anyone, regardless of age or gender. The scarves, which are made from a blend of Australian wool and rayon, come in an array of colours but only one size – long enough to loop around the neck, with plenty to spare.

A curious fusion of architecture and fashion, the *Many Heels* may leave some people scratching their heads in wonder, but that is Yonenaga's goal. 'We always try to redefine what "clothes" are', he explains.

045

MEGAPHONE
Shin Azumi // A Studio
2005 // TOA

Plastered with signs, eye-popping neon, chock-a-block buildings and throngs of pedestrians, Japanese cities can be visually overwhelming. Most are unexpectedly easy on the ears, however: car horns rarely blast out, mobile-phone use is restricted and people tend to talk quietly in public places. And yet the country produces some of the most advanced megaphones in the world. 'They are part of the social infrastructure', explains the designer Shin Azumi. While megaphones are used regularly by subway conductors, campaigning politicians and aggressive salespeople, they are also essential emergency equipment.

Since Japan is prone to natural disasters, such as earthquakes, typhoons and tidal waves, megaphones are almost as common as fire extinguishers. Even so, for years their design had remained largely unchanged. Convinced that it was time for improvement, the TOA corporation, a maker of commercial audio equipment and leading megaphone manufacturer, turned to Azumi, the seasoned designer of speakers, microphones and other TOA products. While there was no need to reinvent the wheel, Azumi proposed a fairly radical makeover.

In pursuit of a more user-friendly and aesthetically pleasing instrument, Azumi worked in consultation with TOA engineers to modify and rearrange the megaphone's components. By moving the battery from its usual place behind the horn down into the handle, Azumi redistributed the weight and placed the megaphone's heaviest part right in the hands of its user. 'If the grip and the weight are separated, the megaphone feels heavier', he says. This change also enabled Azumi to update the microphone. Now covered with a sleek plastic mesh instead of perforated plastic, it looks and sounds much better.

Another big change was to the horn itself. Instead of using the usual opaque material, Azumi specified transparent plastic, which maintains visual contact between speaker and audience. 'It is almost as if the object is not there', he comments. Another benefit is that the scratches and dirt that soon mar the traditional white background are practically invisible. For better function and cooler looks, the horn attaches to the megaphone's body, which is of plastic coloured bright red, yellow or grey. 'It's more like sports gear or something that could sell at the Nike store', jokes the designer.

046

MELTE
Keigo Honda // Honda Keigo Design
2010 // Takakuwa Kinzoku

A collaboration between the Tokyo product designer Keigo Honda and the Niigata Prefecture cutlery-making company Takakuwa Kinzoku, the *Melte* is a family of five spoons. Each is designed for a different purpose – scooping sauce, cereal, cup noodles, jam or ice cream – and each has its own unique shape. But, united by the signature white enamel coating, all are lovely to look at and smooth on the tongue.

When Honda first visited the factory, company executives hoped that he would create a sharp new line of stainless-steel cutlery, the firm's bread-and-butter product. After observing the factory's special enamelling technique, however, Honda was inspired to try something different. 'They make enamel cutlery, but its design does not take advantage of this technique', he explains. Most enamelled metal goods are dipped in batches into a pot of coating, but the company's method uses airbrushing to enrobe each piece individually. The result is a high-quality shell that can smooth over even rough edges, which are usually hard to conceal.

When it came to defining the shape of the *Melte* spoons, Honda followed his client's lead, since the firm had plenty of experience making function-appropriate tableware. While the jam spoon had to be small enough to fit inside a narrow jar, the ice-cream spoon required a blunt end to scrape the surface of the frozen treat, and the cup-noodle spoon needed a broad bowl, since soup is sipped from the side of the spoon.

Each piece is made of moulded stainless steel, utilizing the factory's existing production method. Following the application of enamel, the spoons are baked in an oven for fifteen minutes. In typical enamelled wares, the production process stops once the pieces cool, but there is an added step for the *Melte*. Like all enamel spoons, Honda's have a hole at the top of the handle to facilitate the coating process, and daily washing normally causes the hole's exposed metal edge to rust. 'This hole is not for the user but for the production process', explains Honda. He turned a deficiency into an asset by covering the openings with branded beechwood grips that should keep the enamel looking fresh for a long time.

047

MINDBIKE
Takeo Sunami // TSDesign
2010

In Japan, bicycles are ubiquitous: not simply a form of recreation or exercise, they are also a major mode of transport. Eager to see the streets dotted with better-looking bikes, the product designer Takeo Sunami set his sights on creating an easy-to-assemble, streamlined cycle with ecological benefits, too.

Having designed several bikes for the Japanese brand Muji, in 2008 Sunami decided to make a compact city cycle for such densely populated places as Tokyo or London. He envisioned a simple chassis devoid of unsightly joints, and hoped to build with plastic, but when that proved problematic he switched to metal. After reviewing his mock-up, an aluminium manufacturer in Saitama Prefecture agreed to make a prototype. The test ride was such a success that the bike moved into made-to-order production in 2010.

Drawing its components from ten different suppliers, the *Mindbike* is packaged as a kit of parts – three bars and five joints, plus wheels, pedals, a seat and bits and bobs to hold the lot together – that ships easily in a flat box. The bicycle can be assembled in less than an hour, using only an Allen key and a screwdriver.

'Fundamentally, the way of making bikes has not changed in a hundred years', says Sunami. While he had no intention of completely reinventing bicycle design, he knew he could improve on the industry standard by eliminating welded joints, which are inherently weak. Substituting bolted connections allowed Sunami to trade the typical triangular truss frame for a single aluminium beam strong enough to distribute the rider's weight to the wheels.

The sleek silver beams are made with an extrusion process, and are then chemically polished to a brushed finish. Oval in section, they are scored on either side with a deep groove that conceals bolts and brake cables, and also enables cyclists to attach extras, such as a basket at the back or a mobile-phone holder in front, without compromising the bike's elegant appearance.

As well as consuming fewer resources during fabrication than conventional cycles, Sunami's efficient system allows the owner to swap wheels, replace beams and extend the bike's life. But when the *Mindbike* has run its course, the components can be disassembled and, for the most part, recycled.

048

MIZUSASHI
Takumi Shimamura // Qurz
2008 // Asahi Industries

Gardening is practically a national pastime in Japan. The attachment to plant cultivation is rooted in history, stemming from the time when much of the population lived in a house with land near by. Today even apartment dwellers in the heart of Tokyo lavish attention on their plants, whether a single hydrangea in the living room or a cornucopia of greenery on the balcony. Faced with a dearth of scale-appropriate implements, the urban or indoor gardener had, until recently, little choice but to work the soil with full-size trowels and watering cans. But an invitation to collaborate with the fertilizer manufacturer Asahi Industries enabled the product designer Takumi Shimamura to rectify this deficit.

Shimamura first encountered the corporate conglomerate at a design show at which he was exhibiting his *Monacca* bags (page 126), created to revitalize a dying wood-processing plant. Eager to harvest the designer's creativity, Asahi executives invited him to make a product proposal. Shimamura branched out from the company's agricultural endeavours, and the Comore collection of tools for the urban gardener was the result. One of the collection's first pieces was the *Mizusashi* ('watering can').

As Shimamura laments, 'The usual watering can takes up too much space.' Another drawback is that most are made of eco-unfriendly exterior-grade plastic. Shimamura's solution was to create a rectangular container from bamboo, which is sustainable, fitted with a bent, straw-like aluminium spout. The container is about the same size and shape as a 1-litre (1¾-pint) milk carton, so that it can comfortably be grasped with one hand. The slender pot is held horizontally, both to fill it under a tap through the narrow opening in the side and, with a flick of the wrist, to pour water from the spout to satiate thirsty plants. Although it is easily stowed away, Shimamura's watering can is elegant enough to leave out.

The pot began life with a less refined form: Shimamura's first idea was simply to cap a length of bamboo and attach a spout to its gnarly top. But because there was no way to control the stalk's irregular natural form, Shimamura decided on a square tube with rounded corners instead. It took six months to perfect the design, after which the *Mizusashi* went into production at the Souzou bamboo and wood factory in Kaga Prefecture, and on to the market in 2008.

049

MOKA KNIVES
Motomi Kawakami // Kawakami Design Room
2007 // Kawashima Industry

Today, knives from Japan enjoy a stellar reputation around the world. They owe their success to the country's sword-makers, who honed their craft centuries ago. As Kate Klippensteen wrote in her book *Cool Tools* (2006), 'these highly skilled artisans began fashioning knives for the aristocracy when nationwide peace in the Edo Period [1603–1868] slowed the demand for swords'. Motomi Kawakami's streamlined stainless-steel *Moka Knives* bear little outward resemblance to weapons, but they can make mincemeat of any food that crosses their path.

Suitable for Japanese and Western cuisine alike, the set includes five different shapes ranging from a serrated bread-knife to an all-purpose *santoku*, the sharp corner of which is ideal for paring vegetables – a major component of almost every Japanese meal. While the blade profiles differ, the knives share a distinctive appearance thanks to similarly configured handles. Instead of sporting the usual wooden or plastic grip to hold the blade, each *Moka* knife appears as a single piece of steel stretching from the back of its scored handle to the very tip of its double-edged blade. In reality, though, it is assembled from several components, fabricated separately from different types of steel and then welded together.

Convention dictated the shapes of the blades, but Kawakami designed the distinctive handles. Using modelling clay, he moulded the handle to conform to the hand and then added parallel score lines on either side to keep the grip from slipping – a distinctive feature that also adds visual interest.

Another concern was balancing the weight of the handle and the blade. The blade, which is made of high-strength molybdenum vanadium steel, runs the full length of the knife. The handle, which is composed of two press-moulded steel plates, is hollow but hugs the blade. After welding, the plates are trimmed and vigorously buffed by hand until the seams vanish and all the parts blend into one. The polishing is practically an art form, and is the work of skilled craftsmen in Niigata Prefecture. 'There are not many artisans left in Japan who can do this', says Kawakami. But thanks to such companies as Kawashima Industry, the manufacturer of these knives, their services are in demand.

050

124

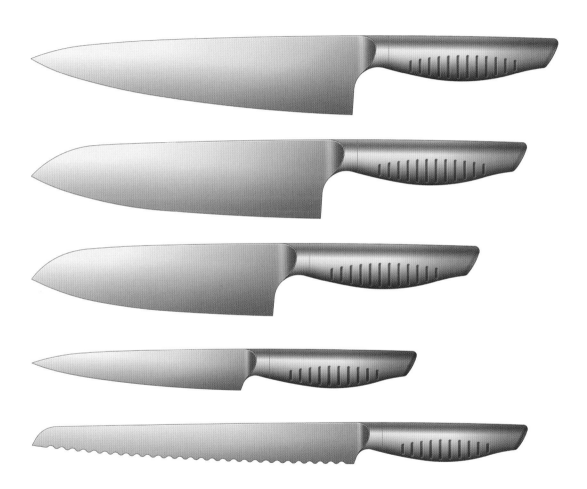

MONACCA
Takumi Shimamura // Qurz
2005 // Ecoasu Umajimura

The wooden *Monacca* bag both resembles and is named after a traditional Japanese sweet consisting of two wafers with azuki bean jam in between (see *Higashiya Monaka*, page 80). Created by the Tokyo designer Takumi Shimamura, the 30 x 46 cm (about 12 x 18 in.) bag is helping to revitalize Ecoasu Umajimura, a wood-processing plant near the designer's home town on the island of Shikoku. The firm specialized in making disposable trays for sashimi from cedar cut down during local forest-thinning, but when business began to dwindle, the factory was threatened with closure.

Eager to assist a local company as well as to chip away at the national problem of waste wood, Shimamura volunteered to design ten prototype products using the plant's moulded wood. The collection, which included objects as diverse as *zabuton* floor cushions, calculators and the *Monacca* bag, was exhibited at Tokyo's Designers Block showcase in 2003. Encouraged by the positive response to the bag, Shimamura asked the company to make 100 of them. When those sold out quickly, the bags went into full-scale production.

Although the composition of each bag was straightforward – two heat-pressed trays treated with polyurethane waterproofing, held together with thick cotton cloth and topped with a leather handle – there were a few construction problems that needed working out. Unsightly folds at the trays' curved corners were a major concern. This problem was alleviated by a pressing technique borrowed from a steel car-part manufacturer Shimamura knew from his automotive-design days. The firm recommended that, instead of shaping a single, thick sheet of wood, very thin (0.5-mm-thick) layers of wood be bent individually and then pressed together.

Poking holes in the wood and stitching it to cloth presented another challenge. 'It is really difficult to sew wood', explains Shimamura. Initially the job was tackled by a company in Saitama Prefecture with heavy-duty machines that stitch together leather golf bags, but eventually Shimamura had special sewing machines made for the production of *Monacca*.

These days Ecoasu Umajimura, which produces some 400 *Monacca* bags every month, is thriving. Yet Shimamura is not ready to stop. 'My dream is to make a mobile phone or a computer [encased] in wood', he says.

051

NEKKO
& Design
2006 // H-Concept

When it comes to flower arranging, every ikebana devotee knows that a single blossom is as beautiful as an entire bouquet – especially when the flower is highlighted by the perfect vessel. Made expressly for a solo bloom, the *Nekko* vase evokes the classic earthenware flowerpot but in an abstract way. The vase has been pared down to basics, consisting of a root-shaped water vial hanging from a thin frame modelled on the terracotta icon. Appropriately named after the Japanese for 'roots', the *Nekko* conceptually reunites the cut flower with its life-sustaining system.

Marketed in collaboration with the design production company H-Concept, the vase was created by & Design, a Tokyo firm founded by four young designers employed by large companies but with a hankering to realize their own ideas. 'If you are working for one maker, you can't design a wide variety of things', explains & Design's Shigenori Ichimura.

The *Nekko* was part of the group's first endeavour, a collection of twelve prototypes that it exhibited at the 100% Design Tokyo trade fair in 2005 (see also *Bird Alarm Clock*, page 46). Unified by the theme of objects straddling two and three dimensions, the collection included pieces as diverse as

wristwatches and light switches. But it was the *Nekko* that attracted the immediate attention of H-Concept.

The vase made its commercial debut in 2006, fundamentally unchanged from the initial mock-up. To emphasize its graphic image, the designers minimized its detailing and thinned its dimensions as much as possible. Yet they had to balance this theoretical agenda with practical functionality and an injection-moulding manufacturing process.

Although the *Nekko* has the look and feel of matt-finished porcelain, it is made of a mixture of plastic and powdered glass, a heavy, durable material that helps to stabilize the narrow vase. A mere 3.35 cm (1⅝ in.) deep and 12 cm (4¾ in.) tall, the *Nekko* is small enough to sit on a windowsill but unlikely to crack if it is knocked over.

A high-tech example of Japan's craft tradition, the vase was carefully constructed to conceal any markings made during its manufacture. The seam at the join of the mould's two halves is cleverly disguised on the inner surface of the frame, and the injection site is hidden at the bottom of the root structure, where only a close inspection is likely to reveal it.

052

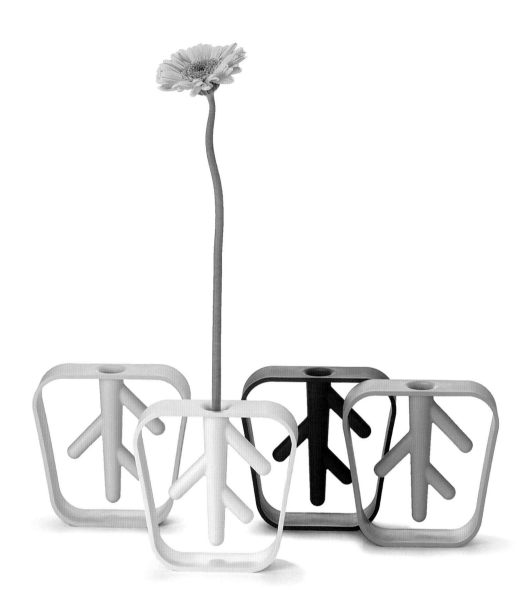

NOOK
Eiji Sumi // DesignWater
2009 // Go Tech

Historically, Seki City in Gifu Prefecture was synonymous with sword-making. Today the city is still a centre for the production of scissors, knives and razors, and many of the area's equipment manufacturers anonymously supply well-known brands with merchandise. Keen to launch a line of its own, Go Tech invited the local product designer Eiji Sumi to create a selection of personal grooming aids made of metal. The *Nook* tweezer – the name is an abbreviated form of the Japanese word *kenuki*, or 'hair removal' – was their first collaboration.

'The body is home to around five million hair follicles, which is a lot of hair to manage', writes Laura Miller in *Beauty Up: Exploring Contemporary Japanese Body Aesthetics* (2006). She goes on to explain that in Japan, a country with a deeply rooted aversion to body hair, it 'suggests a regression from civilization'. According to Miller, men and women in Japan today go to great lengths to get rid of body hair. Despite the availability of an armoury of chemical concoctions, electronic gizmos and other implements to combat this problem, Go Tech was convinced that there was room for a better, safer and more aesthetically pleasing set of tweezers.

Resembling a pair of ice-cream sticks coated with pastel-coloured paint, the *Nook* hardly looks the part. But beneath that benign appearance is a tough set of tongs that can tenaciously grab a single hair. The secret to the *Nook*'s success lies in the spring-like action of its two halves and their roughly textured rounded tips.

The tweezers are constructed in the shape of a wishbone, consisting of two slightly arched stainless-steel strips. Manufactured with a cold-press forging technique, the two pieces are welded at one end and vary in thickness along their length for better movement. They terminate not in the conventional sharp-edged pincers that often catch the surrounding skin, but in flat discs, the surfaces of which are etched with a fine hairline pattern for firm but injury-free hair removal.

After they had developed the *Nook*, the team next created a tool that would cut individual hairs instead of plucking them. Called *Kiir* (from the Japanese verb *kiru*, 'to cut'), the tongs terminate in circular blades. When the two halves are squeezed together, their sharp edges unite and clip the hair in the manner of traditional Japanese scissors, a single piece of bent metal with a sharp, pointed blade at either end.

053

NOON
Yukichi Anno
2007

As every parent of young children knows, cleaning up is a never-ending task, and nowhere is the clutter of toys more of a nuisance than in a small Japanese apartment. This low table with a matching set of building blocks, designed by Yukichi Anno, makes the best of that congested situation, enabling a parent and child to play together and afterwards tidy up the mess in an instant.

Inspired by his home life, Anno created the table when his daughter was one year old so that her bleary-eyed parents would have a place to set down their cups of coffee while she piled the wooden cubes near by. In the manner of a giant ring binder, the rectangular table is divided down the middle by metal rings that hold a movable acrylic sheet. On either side of this spine the two halves of the table are different heights. One side stands 30 cm (nearly 12 in.) tall, perfect either as a Western-style coffee table or as a Japanese-style *chabudai*, the low table used in rooms floored with tatami mats. The other half of the table is several centimetres lower, the ideal height for a toddler to cruise by, stop at and play.

On the lower half of the table, the acrylic sheet is supported by the blocks. When the toys are in use, the sheet can be flipped to the other side, where it is well out of the way; when playtime is over, it turns like the page of a book to cover the blocks and level the tabletop. The clear sheet allows the blocks to be visible at all times, their ever-changing arrangement altering the table's appearance. 'I call it "one day design"', jokes Anno.

A veteran furniture-maker who once worked for a toy company, Anno collaborated on the production of the beechwood table and blocks with a furniture factory in Shizuoka Prefecture. The blocks, which range in shape from cubes and cylinders to triangles and arches, have a long axis of 5.5 cm (just under 2¼ in.). 'This means kids can't eat them', explains the designer. The table's rounded corners are another safety measure, as they limit bumps and bruises, but they also act to soften the table's appearance.

Although Anno worried about the fate of his table once his daughter was beyond the stage of playing with blocks, the *Noon*'s clever design has the capacity to remain useful and fun for many years.

054

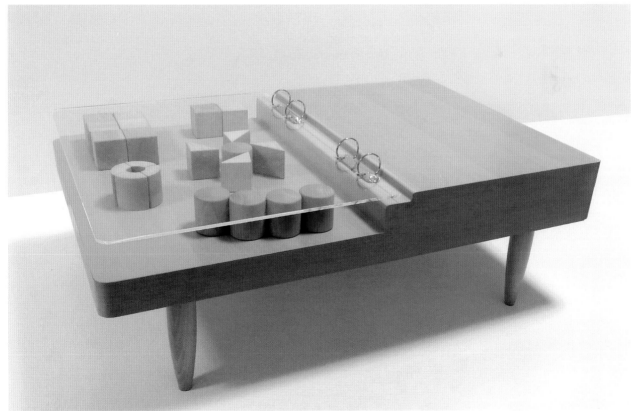

NOTCHLESS
Mamoru Yasukuni // Kikuchi-Yasukuni Architects
2011

Mamoru Yasukuni is not an industrial designer, nor is he an architect. But he is the inventor of the *Notchless*. A squiggle of aluminium that resembles a roll unfurling, this tape dispenser deftly yields strips of sticky tape with a clean-cut edge.

'Ever since my student days, I have been interested in the relationship between form and function', says Yasukuni. Convinced that he could improve the function of the common tape dispenser if he amended its form, he began investigating how to make a version that did not leave zigzag edges. Unsightly and unsanitary, the little corners collect dirt and do not lie flat.

The design of the *Notchless* was a labour of love, taking six years in total. The lengthy process began with the dispenser's cutting teeth. Bettering the conventional jagged profile required a straight cutting edge, but it took fifty attempts for Yasukuni to find the perfect solution: twenty-two incised teeth spaced 1 mm (1/16 in.) apart. And then it took another three years for him to patent his idea.

Once the cutting teeth had been worked out, Yasukuni turned his attention to the body of the dispenser. He began by reconfiguring the standard tape holder. 'Instead of the overall shape, I thought about what would be the best shape for the teeth's function', explains the designer. The result was a 'twin peaks' profile: while a concave 'valley' allows space for fingers to grasp the tape as it comes off the roll, a convex section behind the cutting teeth secures the tape as it is torn.

Many formal decisions grew out of Yasukuni's dialogue with manufacturers. For example, he started with plastic, but that proved to be fraught with problems; through trial and error, Yasukuni concluded that metal was more appropriate. The dispenser body is a single slice of extruded aluminium in which the cutting teeth are incised with an automated drill, and is made at an aluminium factory in Shizuoka Prefecture. A Kanagawa Prefecture company that specializes in clear plastic makes the transparent side plates that secure the roll of tape. The perfectly matched metal and plastic parts snap into place, and the tape is ready to roll.

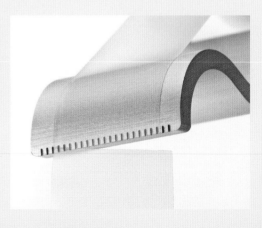

055

NUMBER CUP
Takuya Hoshiko // Design Office FrontNine
2005 // H-Concept

Most people have a favourite number; Takuya Hoshiko, however, adores them all. A product designer with a background in graphics, Hoshiko appreciates numerals' iconic shapes as well as their symbolic meanings. When connected with an anniversary or birthday, some numbers are of significance to individuals. Others carry cultural meaning; for example, in Japan prosperity is associated with the number 8, and renewal with a sixtieth birthday. 'Usually numbers are only seen', says Hoshiko, but the *Number Cup*, a ceramic mini-mug on which a numeral from 0 to 9 serves as the handle, enables people literally to hold a favourite number in their hand.

Sized midway between an espresso cup and a conventional mug, the 160-ml (5½-fl. oz) vessel seems small by Western standards. 'It is about the same size as a handleless cup for green tea, so people [in Japan] are used to it', explains Hoshiko. The cups' simple cylindrical form is indented at the base so that they stack easily for storage – a real plus in the often 'cosy' (tiny) Japanese kitchen. In addition, stacking the cups increases the possible multi-digit numbers exponentially. Convinced that his concept would be well received by gift-buyers, Hoshiko contacted the design production company H-Concept, which quickly agreed to market his clever idea.

The cups are stable and well proportioned, their final form having evolved from numerous trial-and-error studies. Hoshiko had initially envisioned a full-size mug, but discovered that at that scale the numbers could not support their own weight, let alone that of a liquid-filled tankard. In addition to reducing the cup's size, the designer strengthened the bond between cup and handle by modifying the numbers' shapes. The numerals are based on the Helvetica typeface, but some numbers required immediate adjustments, such as attaching serifs, or little projections, to the base of the number 1. Others revealed weaknesses after Hoshiko's paper models became ceramic mock-ups: rendered in clay, the number 2 could not hold its shape until the designer thinned its curved top and thickened its base.

To fuse handle and cup, Hoshiko drew from his furniture-making days by specifying joints in a tongue-and-groove style – a secure but labour-intensive solution requiring hand-assembly at the factory in Gifu Prefecture. But all this effort is well concealed by the cups' glossy white or matt black glaze.

056

NUMBER MEASURING SPOONS
Atsuhiro Hayashi
2012 // Toyo Aluminum Ecko Products

Icy rectilinear slabs of clear acrylic resin engraved with bold recessed numerals, the *Number Measuring Spoons* not only quantify cooking ingredients, but also look cool while doing so. In common with the typically round-bowled conventional measuring spoons, the set includes the three standard Japanese sizes: 15 ml (½ fl. oz), 5 ml (1 teaspoon) and 2.5 ml. However, the spoons have no bowl in which to hold the designated amount of liquid or powder; rather, the numbers themselves act as containers.

The spoons are the product of Atsuhiro Hayashi, an experienced kitchenware designer and an enthusiastic cook. It was cookery-book instructions that gave him the idea of using the forms of numbers for the scoops. 'I was inspired by words like "1 large, 15 ml spoon of salt" or "1 small, 5 ml spoon of vinegar" used in recipes', he explains. 'I wanted to embody and visualize these words.'

The kitchen-goods company Toyo Aluminum Ecko Products deemed Hayashi's concept a clever, marketable idea, and agreed to put the spoons into production. They were all made with an injection-moulding process. However, although they are identical in form and stackable, they vary in thickness: because the numerals are of the same font size, depth is the variable that determines the volume of each spoon – the 2.5-ml model is the shallowest, the 15-ml one the deepest. Looped together by a ring, the spoons add up to one tidy block that stores as easily in a kitchen drawer as it does hanging from a wall-mounted hook.

The *Number Measuring Spoons* have other benefits: being straight and smooth, their edges can level off dry ingredients with one stroke, and in addition the grip of the large spoon has a built-in pasta measure that is equally suitable for spaghetti or soba noodles. The spoons were designed for the Japanese home cook, and therefore their capacities differ slightly from the standard British and American teaspoon and tablespoon, yet their highly functional good looks might make cooks around the world envious.

057

OISHI KITCHEN TABLE
Hisae Igarashi // Igarashi Design Studio
2005 // Fukuchi

Japan's plethora of architectural and interiors magazines might lead one to believe that the country's kitchens always look pristine, but they can be just as messy as kitchens might be anywhere else. 'Newspapers, snacks, games ... there is always something on the table', comments Tokyo-based interior and product designer Hisae Igarashi. Hoping to resolve this problem, Igarashi created a table that practically tidies itself. Instead of one tabletop, it has two; together they sandwich a slot of space in which the flotsam and jetsam of daily life can be stowed in less time than it takes to make a cup of instant ramen noodles.

The table is part of the Oishi ('delicious') Kitchen project, a series of kitchen goods created by independent designers for factories based in Fukui Prefecture. Igarashi was invited to participate by the 'design producer' (see page 20) Toshihiko Sakai, who organized the project. While the theme of quick cleaning was a given, the table's form was Igarashi's unique interpretation.

The table comes in three different shapes in order to fit various room sizes and family configurations. The largest table measures 1.8 m in length (a little under 6 ft) and has an organic form reminiscent of a grand piano (see opposite); while its straight side can align with the wall, its curvy side faces the room's open space. 'People can gather here easily since there are no corners', explains Igarashi. Indeed, while the table comfortably accommodates six people, its wide end is spacious enough for a parent and child to sit together and do homework, whereas its narrow end is ideal for a solo tea drinker.

Igarashi looked closely at the table's impact on its surrounding space. 'Most Japanese rooms are rectangular,' she says, 'but a rounded table can change their character.' A commanding presence in a room of any shape or size, the table has a very solid appearance. Yet beneath its veneer of Japanese ash is a core of paulownia wood, a strong but lightweight material long used in Japan for furniture-making. Two pairs of sturdy L-shaped boards support the top layers. Once belongings have been tucked away in the space between the two tabletops, they may never budge again, but a tidy, inviting table is surely worth that risk.

058

OJUE
Chiaki Murata // Metaphys
2010 // Cube Egg

In Japan, the filling of a bento lunch box is practically an art form. These exquisitely arranged, careful compositions of prepared foods are savoured not just by schoolchildren but by adults, too. Catering to this market are lunch boxes to suit everyone, from people with a taste for Hello Kitty to those who prefer high-end lacquer. Despite the plethora of available styles and shapes, Chiaki Murata of Metaphys identified an unmet need for a slim, upright bento box. His solution? The *Ojue*, a set of three stacking containers secured together by an adjustable band.

Named after a historic stacking box used to present the special cuisine of New Year celebrations, the *Ojue* was not a revolutionary reinvention, but its slim profile and vertical orientation have been improving the lives of office workers, students and others who carry food from home ever since this bento box came on to the market. The *Ojue*'s most distinctive feature is its thinness. Measuring just 5 cm (about 2 in.) in depth, it is stowed away easily in a briefcase, backpack or tote bag – without creating the usual unsightly bulge.

As is the case with most bento boxes, one large compartment is for cooked rice. The *Ojue* includes two others for *okazu* (assortments of bite-sized chunks of food), plus a cosy slot for colour-coordinated chopsticks concealed on top. A removable holder locks the cutlery in place and doubles as a chopstick rest, an important implement that prevents the tips from touching anything unsanitary. The full stacked set forms almost a perfect square but, depending on appetite, the owner can fill as many or as few of the compartments as he or she pleases.

A collaboration between the designer and the housewares concern Cube Egg of Hyogo Prefecture (see *Pokehashi*, page 152), the *Ojue* is made of microwavable polypropylene. After conducting a marketing survey, Murata selected a range of colours in keeping with the bento box's sophisticated image. Conspicuously absent is Metaphys's signature hue, orange (see *Lucano*, page 112). '[That] colour may match the garnishes, but it just doesn't match rice', says the designer.

059

ONE FOR ALL
Naruse Inokuma Architects
2011 // Sumitomo Forestry

A dramatic centrepiece sized for the typical Japanese dining table, the *One For All* is a 1.2-m-long (nearly 4 ft) wooden platter that can serve up an entire multi-course meal for four all in one go. The product of Naruse Inokuma Architects, the platter consists of a single plane indented with square and circular forms that suggest built-in bowls and plates. Each of these indentations was positioned with the precision of rooms in a building's floor plan.

Professional partners with a growing practice, Yuri Naruse and Jun Inokuma met as architectural students at Tokyo University. Several years after graduation, they had a chance to try their hands at home furnishings when a former classmate and his fiancée commissioned them to create a special something to honour their engagement. After lengthy discussions, the architects proposed a choice of a lampshade or a platter. Their clients chose the former, but the designers wanted to realize the latter as well.

'Since this plate is for people gathering, we wanted a material with warmth, like wood', explains Naruse. The architects did not have to look far for a fabricator, as a timber production and purveying company, Sumitomo Forestry, soon offered its help. In addition to marketing the *One For All*, it introduced the partners to a door manufacturer willing to have a go at making the platter. Realizing the complicated form of the dish was not easy. 'If the gaps had been bigger and the holes all the same, it would have been easier', says Naruse. Using full-scale mock-ups and the dimensions of actual dishes, Naruse and Inokuma created an irregular composition that enhances food presentation. Large hollows at either end hold bigger items, such as spaghetti, sushi or salads; in the centre are smaller dips for side dishes and condiments. The level spaces in between are for bread and other finger foods.

Appearing as a smooth, undulating surface, the platter in fact consists of twenty-five thin layers of maple wood, shaped with a vacuum-press mould and secured with glue, with the middle section reinforced for strength and durability. It was finished with a clear polyurethane coating that should ensure that the *One For All* long remains the centre of the party.

060

PAPER-WOOD
Drill Design
2010 // Takizawa Veneer

A material that combines Drill Design's expertise in both graphics and three-dimensional objects, the *Paper-Wood* also blends the firm's two favourite materials into one. Consisting of sheets of coloured card sandwiched between layers of either lime wood or birch, this fresh take on conventional plywood is economical and infinitely adaptable. 'If you use an interesting material, you do not need a fancy form', explains Yusuke Hayashi of Drill Design. The design studio, a partnership between Hayashi and Yoko Yasunishi, not only creates *Paper-Wood* products but also developed the base material as well.

Paper-Wood has its origins in 2007, when Drill Design began investigating ways in which to improve plywood. Aiming to make it less expensive and more visually appealing, the designers started by interleaving different materials with the thin layers of wood. Slices of acrylic and coloured plastic looked wonderful, but were difficult to cut and not sustainable; the inclusion of special woods, such as white birch from the island of Hokkaido, drove costs up. But coloured card – a wood product in its own right, and familiar to the designers from their graphics work – fitted the bill perfectly.

The *Paper-Wood* is produced by Takizawa Veneer, a plywood specialist in Hokkaido, in laminated sheets measuring 182 x 91 cm (just under 6 x 3 ft). When the dried and trimmed boards are viewed in section, the thick layers of card (made from recycled paper) read as stripes interspersed between the wood plies. The material offers Drill Design variables to manipulate: creating bands of different widths and colour combinations (below, left) enables the designers to turn plywood's mundane edges into decorative elements.

Drill Design was keen to explore the potential of its new material, and began building furniture and household goods with it. Instead of concealing the cut sides, as is often done with conventional plywood, the designers sought to create products that would maximize their exposure. Testaments to the *Paper-Wood*'s versatility and visual appeal include *Kago*, a large basket that looks as if it has been woven from L-shaped ribs laced with lines of colour (below, right), and the *Paper-Wood Stool* (opposite), a simple doughnut-shaped seat perched on four legs in which the colourful cut edges face outwards for all to enjoy.

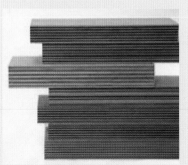
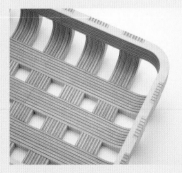

061

PENCUT
Kazuhiro Tsukahara
2009 // RayMay Fujii

The *Pencut* is one of those gadgets that could belong in James Bond's attaché case. With a few swift moves, the fountain-pen lookalike transforms into scissors: a flick of its removable cap reveals a pair of pointy steel blades, and a quick slide of the black catches on either side of its barrel causes loopy handles to emerge. Its moving parts snapped into place, the *Pencut* is set to shear; yet, folded up, it fits neatly into a pen case.

The scissors are the brainchild of Kazuhiro Tsukahara, one of sixteen designers employed by RayMay Fujii, which has been manufacturing writing implements since 1890. The national penchant for pen cases has been around for almost as long. This deeply ingrained habit develops in primary school, when children begin bringing their own writing utensils, and continues on into adulthood. The oblong pen cases, usually made of plastic, cloth or leather, are perfect for toting a few writing tools, but not much else (see also *Red & Blue*, page 156).

For Tsukahara, this limitation was the catalyst for creating a line of compact, pen-shaped stationery goods. A folding pair of compasses that collapses to the size of a ballpoint pen (the *Penpass*) was the first of these products, and the scissors soon followed. Initially Tsukahara had considered adapting Japan's traditional shears, a single piece of bent metal with two blades that cut pincer-style, but he relished the challenge of adapting the pivoted version. The *Pencut*'s steel blades are honed on each side, enabling both right- and left-handed users to cut easily. To prevent slippage while the scissors are in use, the retractable handles slide smoothly and lock firmly. And, finally, the cap closes with a resounding click that audibly indicates that the sharp points are safely covered.

Tsukahara began what turned out to be a year-long design process with a hand-drawn sketch. Many computer-generated drawings and metal moulds later, the *Pencut* was ready for production. Tsukahara chose plastic for the shell because of its low price and weight, and also for the wide colour palette available. 'There is a trend towards more vivid colours in Japan', says the designer, and that explains *Pencut*'s signature hue: an eye-popping turquoise. These good-looking little scissors may not be cut out for a life of espionage, but they suit the Japanese consumer.

062

PLUGO
Masayuki Kurakata // Monos
2007

Japan produces some of the most elegant electronic devices in the world, but in a nanosecond an unsightly extension lead can compromise the aesthetics of even the slimmest television or smallest sound system. To resolve this problem, the product designer Masayuki Kurakata decided to create a lead as beautiful as the appliances it electrifies.

Kurakata's doughnut-shaped device is both an AC 100-volt extension lead and a multi-plug receptacle, and is aptly named *Plugo*, in reference both to its function and to its form. He chose the circular shape because he liked the positive association it carries in Japan, where the word for 'circle', *wa*, also means 'harmony'. Practical considerations led to the circle becoming a ring: while the indented outer edge is the perfect place around which to wrap the lead, the central void enables anyone, young or old, to wind it with one hand. The *Plugo*'s relatively large size (14 cm/5½ in. in diameter) means that when it is not in use it can slide on to the wrist, bracelet-style, to free the hands, or hang on a hook to minimize clutter.

The device consists of two plastic discs that sandwich a recessed groove, in which are enclosed the wiring and the lead. To limit contact with other surfaces and avoid scratches, Kurakata gently tapered each disc's profile, yet the outer edges are thick enough to hold the metal prongs of an electrical plug (unlike in the United Kingdom but as in Europe and the United States, Japanese plugs have two prongs). 'At first I wanted many, many outlets around the perimeter', explains the designer, but he settled for three evenly spaced ports that straddle the ring at its quarter points. The lead is secured by a small clip, and is easily dispatched with a few flicks of the thumb. It culminates in a plastic plug with user-friendly thumb-shaped indentations on either side.

The *Plugo* can extend to 2.5 m (just over 8 ft). This length derives from the average room size in the typical Japanese home: 3.6 x 5 m (nearly 12 x 16½ ft), or eight mats (when it comes to residential space, tatami-mat dimensions still prevail). Half the length of the room's diagonal axis, Kurakata's lead can comfortably connect a corner outlet to an appliance in the centre.

The *Plugo* is available in a choice of seven colours that also acknowledge tradition. While red connotes happiness, muted tones, such as pale green and 'café au lait', meld easily with the understated aesthetics of Japanese interiors.

063

POKEHASHI
Cube Egg
2010

When disposable wooden chopsticks were introduced in Japan in the 1870s, they probably seemed like a good idea. Today the Japanese government estimates that the country consumes some 25 billion pairs each year, as reported by Raju Thakrar in an article titled 'Waribashi: Waste on a Gluttonous Scale' that appeared in Japan Times Online in July 2008. That's a lot of trees. Dismayed by this phenomenal waste, eco-conscious citizens have begun shunning the throwaway utensils and using their own reusable chopsticks instead. The portable, pocket-ready *Pokehashi* (the name merges the first syllable of the word 'pocket' with the Japanese word for 'chopsticks') caters to this crowd.

The set comes swaddled in a canvas 'envelope' modelled on the egg-roll wrapper, and consists of two collapsible chopsticks and their plastic holder. The two halves of each chopstick lock together with a satisfying pop, and the holder doubles as a chopstick rest that stops the mouth-bound tips from touching the tabletop – an absolute taboo in Japan. At the end of the meal, the chopstick halves separate easily for washing and then reuse. This carefully considered product was one of the first created by Cube Egg, a small housewares concern founded in 2009 by Takayuki Sasaki, but was developed by an independent design firm under Cube Egg's aegis. The *Pokehashi* is manufactured in Japan, where Sasaki was certain to get the attention to detail and manufacturing quality he hungered after. 'We wanted to make chopsticks that would be easy to use and [would last] for a long time – that's the true meaning of eco-friendly', he says.

One of the sticking points in the design was the join between the two halves of each chopstick, which needed to satisfy Sasaki's criteria for durability, security and easy assembly. In the finished product, the top and bottom halves lock together seamlessly thanks to spiralling threads on one half and matching grooves on the other. The parts had to be made of different materials: a hard nylon for the top, and polystyrene with fibreglass for the bottom. 'In Japan, we cut hamburgers with chopsticks', explains Sasaki. 'If the material [used to make the chopstick] is too soft, the chopstick would bend as you cut.' But, thanks to the *Pokehashi*'s squared tips and matt finish, these chopsticks work just as well with slippery noodles.

064

RECONSTRUCTION CHANDELIER
Kouichi Okamoto // Kyouei Design
2011

The *Reconstruction Chandelier* is a star-shaped cluster of lights individually encased in glittery gold-plated wires. Looking nothing short of regal, the hanging fixture elevates the lowly industrial-grade cage lamp to candelabra status, but does so without losing sight of the lamp's humble beginnings.

The electric cage lamp has a long history that began in the early twentieth century, and its design is essentially unchanged since its invention. The lamp is intended to illuminate even the darkest and dingiest workspace. Its most distinctive feature is the wire cage that encloses and protects the light but also opens in the manner of a flower at one end for a quick bulb change. At the other end of the lamp is a clamp, enabling easy attachment to just about any protuberance.

'I remembered seeing those lamps as a child', says Kouichi Okamoto, the designer of *Reconstruction Chandelier*. True to his inclination to rework existing objects into something new (see also *Honeycomb Lamp*, page 88) and intent on infusing the old-fashioned cage lamp with new life, Okamoto purchased a few and began reconfiguring them in his studio in Shizuoka Prefecture. His first experiment resulted in a simple table lamp, the *Reconstruction Lamp* (2010), in which a reworked clamp base stands the cage lamp on end. The success of that product led Okamoto to begin to study ways of combining multiple cage lamps.

Initially Okamoto melded the clamp ends with a press mould, since this had worked well for the table lamp. But when that method yielded a less than satisfactory result, he welded the bottoms of twelve lamps together. To complete the process, Okamoto took his creation to a metal-plating company. This factory normally works with car parts, but it agreed to dip Okamoto's entire fixture in 14-carat gold. That didn't do the trick, however: the colour was too brown for Okamoto. So he upped the ante and had the fixture replated, this time with 24-carat gold. 'When I got the bill I was shocked', he exclaims. Although the *Reconstruction Chandelier* is priced for a king or queen, it can be ordered by anyone who can afford to pay for it.

065

RED & BLUE
Yuruliku
2006

Everyone carries a pen case in Japan. Students do it. 'Salarymen' do it. Even old ladies do it. The well-established habit may be a hangover from primary-school days, when most pupils acquire their first pencil pouch. Even today, children are expected to bring their own writing utensils to school. Although many kids favour fancy lead holders over the classic wood pencil, no school set is complete unless it includes a special tool for corrections: an old-fashioned pencil with red lead at one end and blue at the other. The *Red & Blue* is a cylindrical pencil case that takes its cue from this icon; it may have space for only three pens, but it is loaded with nostalgia.

The case, which plays with the themes of memory and longing, is just one of the many stationery and stationery-inspired products created by the design duo Yuruliku. The line-up includes tote bags modelled on notebooks and pillows in the shape of protractors. 'Everyone uses stationery, so it is an easily understood design source', explains Yuruliku's Koushi Ikegami.

From their combined office–studio–shop overlooking Tokyo's Kanda River, Ikegami and his partner, Kinue Oneda, design and fabricate many of their own products right on site. Those they do not make themselves they outsource to small companies and workshops that still exist in Tokyo. The *Red & Blue* is produced by a local bag-maker, which they discovered thanks to a thorough combing of the telephone directory. 'Most of these small makers do not use the internet', explains Ikegami.

The creation of the case was strictly 'old school'. The evolution of its design and various production decisions were based on face-to-face dialogue, and this dovetailed nicely with Yuruliku's tactile design approach. The pair have a strong feel for fabric, and selected the material for the case before deciding anything else. Artificial leather, which is durable and available in a multitude of reds and blues, was the perfect choice. Using a paper pattern and a home-made sample, the designers explained their idea to the fabricator.

It took a lot of back-and-forth to get the shape of the case exactly right, the top zip perfectly aligned down the centre and the nylon lining sewn into place. The finished product enables everyone to carry a little bit of childhood with them.

066

RETTO
Noriko Hashida // Noriko Hashida Design
2010 // Iwatani Materials

In Japan, there is body washing and then there is bathing: the two are completely distinct concepts, and never the twain shall meet. Scrubbing is required before soaking, and it usually takes place at a tap or shower mounted on a wall away from the tub, allowing people to sit on a low stool and wash thoroughly with the aid of a hand-held basin. In recent years the traditional wooden stool and basin have been edged out by nondescript plastic models. Noriko Hashida, who has worked as an in-house designer at a plumbing-fixture manufacturer, knew that she could do better.

Hashida was well acquainted with the ins and outs of tubs and toilets, but started the stool project by conducting internet surveys and physical experiments. With the precision of a scientist, she polled 700 people about their bathing habits and probed the sitting styles of her students at Tokyo's Shibaura Institute of Technology. 'Because we sit naked on bath chairs, my students had to wear loincloths during the experiment', she explains. The result was the *Retto High Chair*,

released in 2010 by Iwatani Materials, which had already produced one bath set designed by Hashida.

The seat functions as a stool but resembles a chair. Supported by front and back panels with wrap-around edges rather than by legs, it has a square bottom that segues into a low seat back. The overall geometry complies with the current trend for straight lines in bathroom design, and the raised back adds comfort; it is just high enough to give lumbar support and low enough not to interfere with washing. The seat is partnered by the *Retto Square Pail*, a vessel for holding and pouring water.

The stool and basin are made at Iwatani's factory in Ibaraki Prefecture, of injection-moulded, matt-finished polypropylene. They are easy to clean and keep mould-free – a concern in Japan, where atmospheric humidity runs high. While a slit in the stool's seat acts as a drain, its 'legs' hook over the side of the bath, enabling the stool to drip-dry out of the way when not in use.

067

RIPPLES
Toyo Ito // Toyo Ito & Associates, Architects
2003 // Horm

As its name suggests, the *Ripples* bench was inspired by the image of rocks thrown into a river. Its smooth surface is animated by indented circles that indicate individual seating places. Equally at home in residential and non-residential settings, the bench is a collaboration between the Japanese architect Toyo Ito and the Italian furniture company Horm.

The *Ripples* carries strong echoes of the floor plan of Sendai Mediatheque, a library-cum-community centre designed by Ito and completed in 2001, in which the primary space-defining elements are the massive, irregularly placed tubular columns that puncture its rectangular plan. When Ito was invited to create an outdoor bench for Tokyo's Roppongi Hills mixed-use development, he drew from his earlier idea, albeit at a much smaller scale.

The first *Ripples* bench was made of architectural steel and concrete, which reflected the materials used in nearby buildings, and its water image was Ito's poetic response to the tree-lined avenue beside which the bench was sited. Ito's concept inched closer to the forest when the bench was reborn in wood after a meeting with Luciano Marson, Horm's founder, in Italy in 2002. As Erica Nespolo of Horm relates, Marson asked Ito: 'Why don't we bring it to life?'

Their project took off in 2003 with a limited edition of 100 benches, each made of six layers of different woods laminated together. The bench went into serial production in 2006. To differentiate the two versions, the serial bench consists of only five layers – walnut, mahogany, ash, cherry and oak – that form the bench's 3-cm-thick (nearly 1¼ in.) seating surface. Using a computer numerical control machine, Horm's artisans make the initial circular cuts through the layers, revealing the various grains and colours of the woods; their beauty is highlighted after hand-sanding and oiling, when the different layers meld into one flowing, continuous surface.

The rounded recessions are placed in an artful but irregular arrangement. '[They're] like the multiple tubes in Sendai', explains Ito. But they also align from bench to bench, yielding a potentially endless stream of *Ripples*.

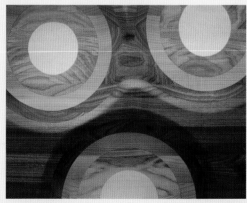

068

ROCK
Jin Kuramoto // Jin Kuramoto Studio
2009

This exquisite crystalline flower vase evokes the spirit of nature but is made of pure acrylic. The product of Jin Kuramoto, the *Rock* grew out of the designer's desire to replicate a landscape of horizontal rocky outcroppings punctuated by vertical plant shoots. It was a departure from the stark white forms, often based on Platonic solids, that characterize many of Kuramoto's earlier works, and it catapulted the designer's career in a new direction. 'With this project, I changed my design style', he explains.

The recipient of a design education as well as on-the-job training at a large electronics company, Kuramoto was well versed in established approaches to the development of new products. 'But design is actually a much freer thing', he comments. 'It was important for me to find my own way.' Liberated from the corporate approach, he pursued a stronger aesthetic expression, looser forms and a zealous use of colour.

All these ideas were present in the *Rock* from its inception. Instead of starting with an image of a single vase, Kuramoto envisioned an entire scene composed of rock forms piled one on top of the other.

From there he excavated individual pieces, first through sketches and then through hand-carved models. Kuramoto's 3D data became the basis of prototypes realized by a factory in Kanagawa Prefecture, which carefully cut each one to the designer's detailed specifications.

The vase prototypes were produced in three sizes, the longest being 18 cm (just over 7 in.) in length, but all measure 3 cm (just over 1 in.) in height. They were rendered in red, blue and a multitude of other shades, and each draws the eye as if it were a giant gem. In common with any other stone, it can be appreciated from every direction; there is no discernible front, back or correct orientation. Instead, each faceted side brilliantly reflects light.

By contrast, the bottom and top are level, ensuring that the vases can be stacked comfortably and safely, and that the flowers stand upright. The stems are supported by a built-in *kenzan*, or frog, excised from the surface of the *Rock*. An appealing pattern of parallel strips inspired by clumps of coral, the frog can hold anything from a single stem to an entire ikebana floral arrangement.

069

ROLL
Oki Sato // Nendo
2010 // Flaminia

A dynamic swirl of white glazed ceramic that sits boldly on a counter top, the *Roll* hardly resembles a conventional washbasin. The unique spiral form of this elegant sink encircles water flowing from the tap, holding it for a moment before it runs down the drain. Produced in Italy by the plumbing-fixture company Flaminia and marketed in Japan by Cera Trading, part of toilet-maker Toto, the *Roll* was designed by the Tokyo designer Oki Sato and his firm, Nendo.

Flaminia was introduced to Sato by the architect and furniture entrepreneur Giulio Cappellini, and it commissioned Nendo in 2004 in the hope that its maverick designers would create a sink that was simple but different. 'What [Flaminia] wanted was something poetic but with a pinch of humour', recollects Sato. Taking a novel approach, he envisioned a basin that could capture water, as opposed to the typical sink, which passively accepts water as it descends from the tap.

'I did not start with a bowl, but with a ceramic sheet', says Sato. True to his firm's name (*nendo* translates as 'modelling clay'), the designer approached the assignment as if he were a sculptor. He began by manipulating this ribbon of material, overlapping its ends to contain the water. 'I wasn't creating a form but a gesture', he explains.

To convey his concept, Sato made hand-drawn sketches. 'They were really more like manga', says the designer with a chuckle. Working with one of Nendo's in-house designers, he resolved the details in a matter of weeks. He carefully considered the outline of the curve, as well as the thinness of the rim and how to render in plumbing-grade clay the critical overlap – it could not be too tight or too loose.

Using models and computer drawings made by Nendo, the factory in Italy began producing prototypes with conventional moulds and a kiln-baked process. But because of the sink's delicateness, particular care was required for the casting, drying and, especially, the cleaning and finishing processes. Flaminia introduced the *Roll* at the Milan Furniture Fair in 2010; it is available in two forms, circular (with a diameter of 44 cm/17⅜ in.) and oval (with a length of 56 cm/just over 22 in.).

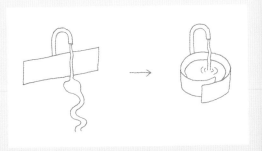

070

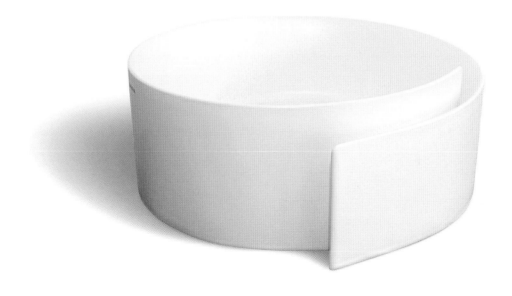

ROUND & ROUND
Shunsuke Takahashi
2010 // Arnest

For the times when they are in use, dish-drying racks are essential to every kitchen. But, in the typically tiny Japanese kitchen, for the remaining twenty or so hours a day they simply take up precious space on the worktop. Shunsuke Takahashi set his mind to doing his bit to ameliorate this problem by designing a drying rack that could be stowed away easily when not needed. His solution was the *Round & Round*, which is produced in Niigata Prefecture by housewares maker Arnest, where Takahashi is a member of the product development department.

In contrast to the conventional box-shaped rack and draining board, Takahashi's creation is a flat, slatted mat that sits right over the sink; when it is not needed, it can be rolled up into a tidy bundle (below), in the manner of the bamboo and cotton-string *makisu* mat used for making rolled sushi. The *Round & Round* is manufactured in China of steel bars coated with silicone dyed fluorescent orange or green – Arnest's signature colours.

In addition to matching the colour scheme of the company's spoons and spatulas and being easy to store, the *Round & Round* has a number of practical attributes. Its brawny steel skeleton can support up to 10 kg (22 lb) of kitchenware, and its forgiving flat shape can accommodate any dish, from the heaviest clay *nabe* for one-pot dishes down to the most delicate sake cup – and all without slippage, thanks to the silicone coating. The gaps between the bars allow air to circulate around wet tableware and for water simply to drip off into the sink; a strip of perforated silicone along one edge holds cutlery and chopsticks.

Takahashi's rack can even act to extend the kitchen work area, since it is strong enough to hold cutting boards or bowls of food over the sink, making it far more versatile than the conventional space-consuming basket rack and tray. But, beautiful and functional as the *Round & Round* is, its best attribute may be its compact, easy-to-store rolled form.

071

SAKURASAKU
Hironao Tsuboi
2006 // 100%

Each spring in Japan, people wait expectantly for the *sakura*, or cherry blossoms, to bloom. As the buds begin to open up, the media charts their progress, fuelling a national flower-viewing frenzy. For the few short days when they are at their peak, the faintly pink flowers completely cover their trees, lifting people's spirits everywhere with their extraordinary but ephemeral beauty.

Modelled on Japan's most celebrated flower, the *Sakurasaku* drinking glass has the distinctive five-petal profile of a cherry blossom in its prime. But, unless viewed from the bottom, the glass does not reveal its special shape until it is filled with a chilled drink and is coated with condensation. A nuisance at best and an enemy of wooden tables at worst, condensation is often countered with a coaster. But by leaving an imprint of a *sakura* blossom, the glass turns a negative into a positive. 'The power of design is that it can change feelings', explains the glass's creator, Hironao Tsuboi.

Instead of starting with the object, Tsuboi began by thinking about the action of repeatedly putting a condensation-coated glass down on a table. He hoped that, by changing the shape of the glass's base from circular to *sakura*, he could change people's perception of the unwanted rings. Starting with a hand-drawn sketch, he quickly advanced to full-scale models made of synthetic wood. Although the design phase lasted only a month or two, it took eighteen months to refine the production process.

The glasses are made of barium crystal glass, a material that is strong even when it is very thin, and are less than 1 mm ($\frac{1}{16}$ in.) thick. They are marketed by 100%, the company Tsuboi founded with his brother, and are manufactured individually and largely by hand in a Tokyo factory that specializes in traditional glassware, and which has the capability to realize Tsuboi's complex form. The glasses come in three sizes – sake, tumbler and rocks – in a choice of clear or a cherry-blossom light pink, but it is their spiritual impact that gives Tsuboi the most satisfaction. As their name ('*sakura* are blooming') reinforces, they are as a dream come true.

072

SEN
Pinto
2011

The *Sen*, which elevates the lowly wire clothes hanger to new aesthetic heights, is so elegant that it seems a waste to cover it with clothes. Titled with the Japanese word for 'line', it is a single, seemingly continuous strand of steel that mysteriously loops round and morphs into a two-pronged hook that grabs on to the wardrobe rail. The product of the design duo Pinto, the *Sen* does not fundamentally alter the hanger's function, nor its classic triangular form, but the designers' fine-tuning and characteristic attention to detail have turned an often-overlooked item into an *objet* that anyone would be glad to have hanging around.

Pinto partners Masayoshi Suzuki and Takanori Hikima, in-house designers at a manufacturer of office furniture and an electronics firm respectively, began collaborating in order to express their own design sensibility. Conversing on Skype after work and occasionally meeting in person at weekends, the duo puts out a themed collection each year. *Sen* is one of six items introduced in Pinto's 'Like It' series, an eclectic assortment loosely unified by the designers' own predilections. 'If you do not make something you like, others probably won't like it either', reasons Hikima.

While the designers had no particular aversion to the overall shape of ordinary hangers, the twisted joint securing the wire end was beyond tolerable. It was simply too busy-looking and had too many lines, and the pair were certain that they could do a better job of sealing the loop more minimally.

After careful study, the designers' solution was to bend both wire ends into hooks and then invisibly weld them together end-to-end. Their theory was that two hooks not only look better, but also function better than one, and the configuration supports even the heaviest of overcoats. The *Sen*'s double hook is beautifully proportioned, with a longer 'neck' than the standard hanger, and a smaller curved 'twin head' that fits snugly around the hanging rail, keeping clothes in line.

Pinto's hanger, which is manufactured by a small steel fabricator in Kanagawa Prefecture, was at first a conventional shade of silver, but that was too reflective for the designers. A quick change resulted in a matt-black finish that quietly highlights *Sen*'s sleek silhouette.

073

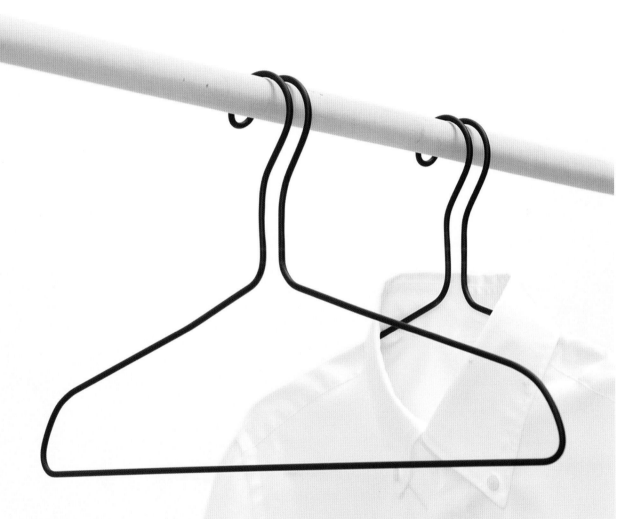

SILENT GUITAR
Yamaha
2001

A 'silent musical instrument' may seem an oxymoron, but in Japan, where houses are very close together and apartment walls are thin, such a thing can be a godsend. Thanks to Yamaha's *Silent* series, musicians of various types can play to their heart's content without worrying about disturbing others or causing complaints from neighbours.

Electric instruments, in which sound is created by electric signals, have been around since the early twentieth century. In the early 1990s Yamaha introduced hybrid versions that can both generate acoustic sound and amplify it electronically, starting with the *Silent Piano*. Its *Silent Guitar*, launched in 2001 and upgraded several times since then, comes complete with wooden fingerboard, nylon strings and, thanks to a rim of black plastic, the guitar's iconic figure-of-eight outline: the standard points of interface between player and instrument are present. But the large resonation box that forms the body of the acoustic instrument and generates its sounds is absent; in its stead, a pick-up system beneath the base of the fingerboard senses vibrations generated by strumming the strings and transmits them to an amplifier. By using headphones, musicians can play as loudly as they please. If they want a gentle sound, the guitar can be played unplugged. 'It is about one-tenth the sound volume of a regular guitar', says Manabu Kawada, general manager of Yamaha's Product Design Laboratory.

While duplicating the feel of playing and the sound quality of an acoustic guitar was the priority, the design of the *Silent Guitar* was as much a process of elimination as one of creation. 'We thought about what parts of the instrument the player needs and does not need', explains Kawada. In addition to removing the unnecessary, the team made some improvements: the bottom of the frame is equipped with a wooden rest that sits comfortably on the thigh, and the instrument's detachable top makes it easier both to carry the guitar and to store it when practice time is over.

The *Silent Guitar*, which visually echoes a classic Gibson model, distils the instrument to its essence, and, in the manner of a classical Japanese painting, omits the superfluous. With minimal means it meets Japan's challenging physical conditions.

074

SKIP
Takanori Hayakawa // C.H.O. Design
2008 // Kokuyo Furniture

Until recently, people's concept of office work consisted of commuting to a workplace and sitting at a desk, but the arrival of laptops and other portable electronic devices is changing this attitude. 'Now you can work anywhere – inside, outside, or even at the park', explains Takanori Hayakawa. A product designer who often brainstorms with companies about ideas for future products, Hayakawa created the *Skip*, a prototype of a workstation on wheels, for an in-house exhibition of advanced design hosted by Kokuyo Furniture.

The movable desk enables desk drones to whizz round the office, leaving conventional cubicles in the dust. It consists of a work surface sized for little more than a laptop, plus a stool-like seat capped with an upholstered cushion, with the two parts integrated into a single metal chassis that rests on four wheels. With a gentle, scooter-style kick or two, *Skip* users can roll here and there for an impromptu meeting with colleagues, a pit stop at the water cooler or a simple change of scene – all without ever leaving their desk.

A designer with a knack for reinventing daily objects and combining functions in unprecedented ways, Hayakawa initially envisioned the *Skip* as a giant tricycle (below). 'My first idea was a bike plus a desk, but this concept evolved into a desk that moves', he explains. Plywood was Hayakawa's original material of choice, because it is relatively lightweight (hence mobile) and durable, but cost concerns drove him towards steel instead.

The *Skip* measures 75 cm (29½ in.) in height – the standard desk height in Japan – and, instead of having a simple rectangular form, is indented both front and back; this shape not only eliminates unwanted build-up of stress at the outer edges of the desk and seat, it also adds to the *Skip*'s streamlined appearance. Although its design is finalized, and it has been fabricated by a metalworker who regularly builds prototypes for Hayakawa, the *Skip* has yet to go into production.

075

SLEEPY
Daisuke Motogi // Daisuke Motogi Architecture
2010

When it comes to sleeping, nothing can compare to bedding down on a futon mattress fresh from airing in the sunshine; it brings the sweetest dreams and the most restful sleep. 'Everyone in Japan has strong memories of this experience', says architect and designer Daisuke Motogi. The *Sleepy*, the project that launched Motogi's solo practice, was created to capture that feeling, but in chair form.

Among its various attributes, the typical futon is a very flexible piece of furniture that becomes a bed at night but can be folded up and stowed away in a specially designated deep closet during the day. This enables private sleeping quarters to become communal areas, and frees up scarce floor space in Japan's typically tiny homes; but it presents a problem for afternoon nap-takers looking for a cosy spot in which to put their head down.

The *Sleepy* seat, which mimics the shape of a folded futon, is the solution, as it creates the ideal place for a quick shut-eye. The prototype, manufactured by a furniture fabricator in Tokyo, consists of a futon-shaped cushion folded over a wooden base padded with thick wads of cotton to smooth over its sharp corners. Both top and bottom are swaddled with a white cover as soft as cotton bedlinen, and they are attached to each other by strips of Velcro tape.

The seat's most critical component is the folded top. Getting its form exactly right – it had to replicate both the look and the comfort of a futon – required the testing of many configurations and distribution of different filling materials. Concealed by the uniform cover, the cushion's contents vary along its folded length: the seating element contains a mixture of feathers and cotton, in the manner of a luscious duvet, but the headrest is filled entirely with ethane foam used for pillows. As a final touch, the fabricator's craftsmen permanently sewed into place each of the *Sleepy*'s carefully calibrated folds, ensuring that the fluffy seat is always ready for those in need of a little rest.

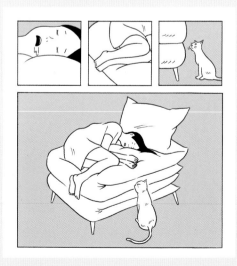

076

SOFT DOME SLIDE
Hisae Igarashi // Igarashi Design Studio
2009 // Jakuetsu

A rounded 1.08-m (3½-ft) 'mountain' or hill articulated with crater-shaped holes, a cave-like tunnel and a gentle slope, the *Soft Dome Slide* is a play structure that invigorates the imagination as much as the body. The structure, which is aimed at two-year-olds, is made by Jakuetsu, a manufacturer of childcare items based in Fukui Prefecture. The company was expanding into the nursery-school market, and contacted the interior designer Hisae Igarashi in the hope that she would try her hand at playground equipment.

At the outset of the collaboration, Igarashi was herself the mother of a small child. 'Two-year olds are between babyhood and childhood', she explains. 'They can run, but their balance is not so good.' The designer's first endeavour was the *Card*, a kit of poles and panels that can be individually configured to match the space of a nursery and the abilities of the children. The *Soft Dome Slide* followed shortly after.

'In Japan, the typical slide is shaped like an animal, such as an elephant with a long trunk,' says Igarashi, 'but I wanted something more abstract.' She imagined a hill instead, and created a hemispherical 1:10-scale styrofoam model, then carved steps at one end, a slide in the other and a tunnel through the middle. 'Kids and animals alike gravitate towards small spaces', comments Igarashi. 'And they love to play hide-and-seek.'

While it was desirable to give children a modicum of physical challenge, safety was Igarashi's paramount consideration. To prevent bumped heads and unexpected falls, she adjusted the width of the steps and the splay of the slide, and scooped out a side section of the dome so that adults can stand near their wobbly wards as they ascend. While this last revision shortened the length of the tunnel, it yielded a multifaceted play structure in which kids' creativity rules.

Safety was a critical factor in choosing the material, too. The structure needed to be neither too soft nor too hard, and neither too slippery nor too rough, and it had to stand up to both indoor and outdoor conditions; a combination of rubber-like polyurethane and urethane was the ideal choice. Unlike Igarashi's *Card*, once the *Soft Dome Slide* has been fabricated in a mould (in a range of three pastel colours: pink, blue or green), it is playground-ready.

077

SPIN
Flask
2005 // Yamauchi Spring

Delicate and ethereal, the *Spin* is barely a basket, let alone a fruit bowl, and yet the coil of impossibly thin steel wire is capable of supporting any fruit, from plums to pineapples. Designed by the Flask partnership (now dissolved), the *Spin* puts bounce into the industrial products made by Yamauchi Spring.

The Fukui Prefecture company has manufactured springs of all sizes since 1947, but had never before worked with an outside product designer. Its collaboration with the avant-garde Tokyo-based designers started after the local government consulted the product designer Toshihiko Sakai (see page 36) about ways in which to support the area's industries. 'They believed that good design would yield good sales', explains Sakai, who agreed to pair local businesses with innovative product designers.

Flask's partners, Naoko Matsumoto and Ryuichi Sato, were new to the world of spring-making, so they began by visiting Yamauchi's factory to familiarize themselves with the company's products and manufacturing capabilities. 'We wanted to use Yamauchi's existing technology', says Matsumoto, who

favoured this cost-conscious strategy. But Flask also wanted to use spings to make something new and exciting.

A fruit bowl fitted the bill. Essentially a single spring, the *Spin* consists of a 7-m-long (nearly 22 ft) wire that spirals round a thick central steel ring. Small slits in the ring hook the wire into place, eliminating the need for expensive welding, while a tiny spring normally used in eyewear frames joins the ends of the wire, turning it into a continuous loop. 'It looks a little like a bicycle wheel', comments Matsumoto. The tray-like form consists of twenty-seven wedge-shaped loops that radiate from the centre ring. While the loops' inward slant keeps fruit from sliding off, their assembly allows air to circulate freely among the apples, bananas and oranges. 'We wanted the image of fruit floating on a plate', says Matsumoto.

Minimalist yet mighty, the *Spin* can comfortably hold eight to ten fruit. 'That's the usual amount you would put on a table', according to Matsumoto. But even the heaviest fruit look as if they are supported purely by air.

078

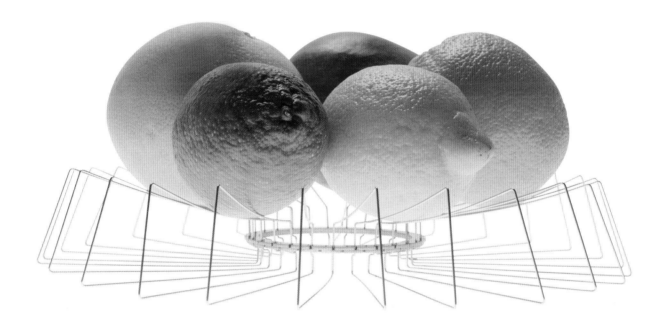

SPLASH
Yasuhiro Asano // Asano Design Studio
2003 // H-Concept

The *Splash* umbrella stand reflects its purpose through its shape, which mimics a raindrop hitting the pavement, but it has a sunny disposition. While the rubber receptacle's compact, sinuous form does its duty by holding up to twelve umbrellas, its bright colours and playful shape brighten up any home or business foyer.

A collaboration between design production company H-Concept and product designer Yasuhiro Asano, the umbrella holder began as Asano's submission to a competition for aluminium products hosted by Toyama Prefecture in 2000. Searching for a form that would look good even when not in use, and aiming to provide separate but equal areas for wet and dry umbrellas, Asano started by investigating geometric shapes that had no distinct front or back. Continuous loops met his criteria, since they can grip umbrellas on either side.

Once he had settled on the stand's overall configuration, Asano sculpted a styrofoam mock-up and encased it in sand to make a mould for molten aluminium. 'It was a very complicated process', he says. The resulting tapered pot ringed with eight lobes won an award, but because the sand left impressions on the container's surfaces that were scratchy enough to make rips in umbrella tops unless painstakingly polished by hand, the prototype was essentially unmarketable – until its rediscovery by H-Concept.

The aluminium umbrella holder caught the eye of H-Concept's director, who ferrets out good design ideas, fabricates them locally and puts the finished product on the market. In the prototype he saw a potentially big seller, but it needed a few tweaks.

Cutting the stand's height in half and reducing the number of lobes to six multiplied its versatility. Trading its tapered profile for a vertical one streamlined the manufacturing process. And replacing the aluminium with rubber, which can be dyed in various colours, gave the umbrella holder a fresh, fun image.

After H-Concept had added the finishing touch in the form of a catchy name, Asano's new and improved umbrella stand was ready to enter production at a rubber factory in Saitama Prefecture. The stand made a big splash, and was an instant success.

079

STAND
Genta Kanayama // Genta Design
2005 // Duende

According to the product designer Genta Kanayama, the average Japanese person consumes a whopping thirteen boxes of paper tissues a year – more than any other nationality in the world. Disposable tissues are among the necessities of daily life, and no room is complete without a stash of its own. But in Japan's typically tiny homes, those oblong cardboard boxes take up valuable space. Intent on saving centimetres and improving interior aesthetics, Kanayama set his mind to the task, and this vertical dispenser, aptly named *Stand*, is the result.

Disposable tissues were introduced in the United States in 1924, but did not arrive in Japan until the 1960s, when all things Western were deemed modern and, therefore, desirable. Initially they were an expensive luxury, but as their price dropped, tissue usage rose, and it overtook American consumption in 1978. 'Today the cost of tissue in the United States is three times higher and in England seven times higher [than in Japan]', says Kanayama, a self-taught expert on tissues.

Using the geometry of Japan's standard rectangular box as his starting point, Kanayama simply set the container on end. Although this vertical position took up much less surface area than the horizontal one, it severely compromised the box's stability. Kanayama remedied this by encasing the cardboard box in a stainless-steel shell that broadened into a curved flange at its base. An opening in the bottom enabled the tissue box to be slid in cartridge-style, while single sheets billowed out through a slot on the front.

This prototype debuted in 2004 during Tokyo Designers Week, where it caught the attention of the talent scout for design production company Duende, Koji Nishiba. But Kanayama's design needed a few modifications to improve its manufacture and marketability. Straightening the curved base strengthened the box's aesthetics considerably, and also reduced production costs. To cut the price even further, Kanayama and Nishiba decided to fabricate in plastic rather than steel.

Made in Taiwan by an injection-moulding process, the dispenser was launched in a choice of four colours. In order to fuel consumer interest, Duende expanded the line by releasing the *Stand* in different hues, and in steel and wood versions. 'People always expect something new when they visit shops', explains Nishiba. Although colours may come and go, Kanayama's timeless design is destined to stay.

080

STANDING RICE SCOOP
Marna
2009

A tool tailored expressly for scooping rice from its cooking vessel, the *shamoji* is an essential utensil in any Japanese kitchen. The flat paddle is traditionally made of wood, bamboo, ceramic or lacquerware, and has taken its form from its function. While the introduction of electric rice cookers after the Second World War spawned smaller plastic scoops, the basic utensil remained largely unchanged for more than a century. But when a customer of the Tokyo-based housewares manufacturer Marna requested a case in which to keep the scoop clean as well as close to the cooker, the firm's design team began reconsidering the iconic form.

Marna's designers reasoned that a freestanding scoop would eliminate the need for a case altogether. Inspired by the razor-like profile of a Japanese sword, they devised an ultra-thin paddle that slips easily through cooked rice. 'If rice is smashed, it loses its taste', explains Marna's Takayuki Inoue. In addition, embossed dots keep the sticky cooked kernels from adhering to the scoop. Viewed in profile, the spoon has an overall S-shape, the curved top and bottom balancing each other, and the wide, wedge-shaped base enabling the scoop to stand upright on any worktop or table.

Satisfied with the streamlined form, the team turned their styrofoam mock-up into polypropylene prototypes. They then issued the scoops to Marna employees and sought their feedback. Armed with this information, the designers fine-tuned the handle's shape before proceeding to production, an injection-moulding process at a factory in Japan.

The self-supporting spoon went on the market in 2009 in a choice of black or white plastic. Although white remains customers' perennial favourite, Marna now makes the scoop in an additional six colours, and in 2010 the firm launched a smaller, tapered version; equipped with a pointed tip, it makes it easy to put rice into a Japanese bento lunch box.

081

STEP STEP
Motomi Kawakami // Kawakami Design Room
2008 // Nissin Furniture Crafters

In Japan, exchanging outdoor shoes for indoor slippers on entering the home is a deeply ingrained custom. Its origins lie in traditional houses, where shoes were left in the dirt-floored entrance hall before one stepped into the living spaces. While architecture has changed considerably, the action of changing one's footwear still demarcates the two realms, and it is a practical way of reducing dirt tracked into the home.

Although it is relatively easy to remove one's shoes while standing in the confined space near the door, putting them on often requires something on which to sit, and a shoehorn. It was while donning his own oxfords that the product designer Motomi Kawakami hit on the idea of integrating the two parts into a single piece of furniture. 'Rather than loose-fitting slip-on shoes, I personally prefer to wear smart-looking, lace-up shoes', explains the designer. 'For this reason, whenever I go out, I sit down on a chair, use a shoehorn to put on my shoes and then lace them up.' His *Step Step*, a wooden stool with a slot at the back to hold its matching shoehorn, is perfectly tailored to that need. A far cry from the upholstered seating and high-tech office chairs that Kawakami routinely produces (among other objects; see *Moka Knives*, page 124), the simple but graceful stool was created under the aegis of the Japan Design Committee's 'Furniture for a Personal Use' project.

The programme, which promoted the skills of makers of wooden furniture in the Hida Takayama area of Gifu Prefecture, paired six committee members with local fabricators and asked each designer to create an item suited to his or her own lifestyle. The parts for Kawakami's whimsical stool are made by Nissin Furniture Crafters of richly grained walnut, beech or oak, and are easily assembled by the customer, as no tools are required to fit the four angled legs into the circular seat. The shoehorn hangs from a hole at the back, out of the way yet within easy reach, with its scooped blade dangling below the seat and its knobbly top rocking back and forth above. As though it were a hand waving, the *Step Step* stool warmly greets its owners as they come and go.

082

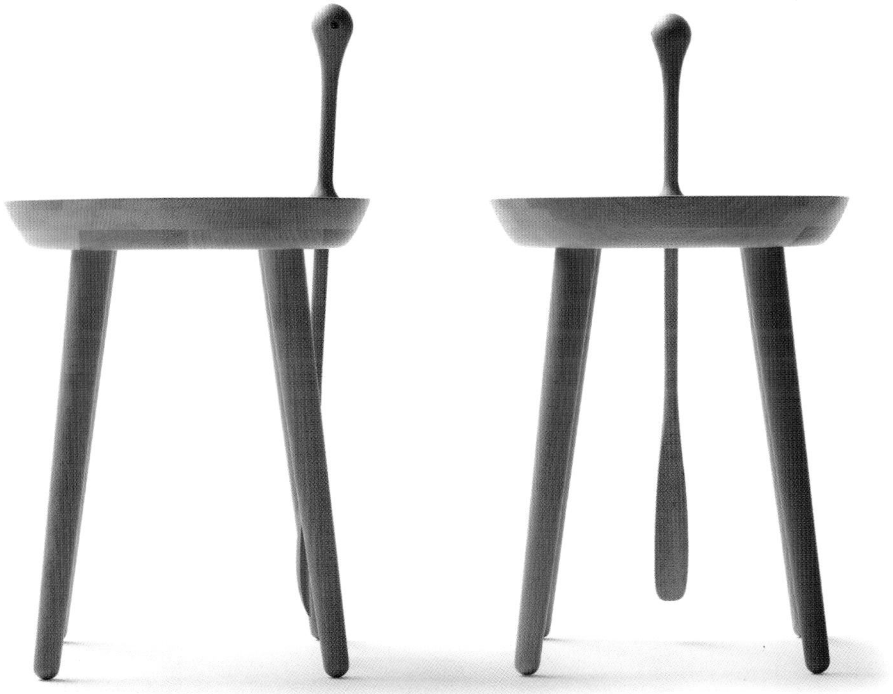

SUSPENCE
Shigeru Aoki
2009 // Arnest

The eye is attracted to these blocks of brightly coloured plastic pegs, and curiosity is awakened. But as regards function, the *Suspence* keeps one guessing. The only clue is the word 'pen' hidden inside its name: combining two uses in one object, the unique *Suspence* is a pair of bookends that double as pen holders. Steel plates on the bottom of each block help to secure books in place, and orderly arrays of pegs on top grasp pens, rulers, postcards and the like.

The *Suspence*, which is manufactured by housewares producer Arnest, is the brainchild of Shigeru Aoki, one the company's thirteen in-house designers. Arnest's president, Kunio Suzuki, is drawn to products with ambiguous shapes, and he responded favourably to Aoki's initial proposal. As Aoki explains, 'Japanese people often use pens when they are reading.' His colleague Ken Kikuchi continues: 'That's when new ideas frequently come up. They are like streaming water, so we must write them down immediately.' This national proclivity inspired Aoki to bring books and pens together.

The designer's first rendition of the *Suspence* was almost the exact inverse of its final form. He had envisioned not individuated pegs but solid blocks pierced by holes that would hold pens, but even he found this shape boring and its function limited. The substitution of solid cores for the void holes was a great improvement. No longer restricted by the holes' geometry, the product could hold all sorts of items between its tentacles.

Aoki refined his product bit by bit, progressing from drawings to scale models made of laser-carved plastic. Because the *Suspence*'s plastic base is quite light, the designer needed an L-shaped metal plate for stability and to secure the books. Although he kept the height of the pegs uniform, he varied the depth of the pockets in between: shallow for writing implements, and deeper for envelopes or postcards. He also studied the distance that was needed between pegs in order to keep pens and paper in place.

Once the details were resolved, the *Suspence* moved into injection-moulding production. Aoki had hoped that this could be achieved with two injection points, but the factory in China had to inject each peg separately, leaving the top of each one with a dot-like impression or 'scar'. This happy accident led Aoki to cap the pegs with covers of a contrasting colour, bringing to mind images of felt-tip markers and visually hinting at the *Suspence*'s intended purpose.

083

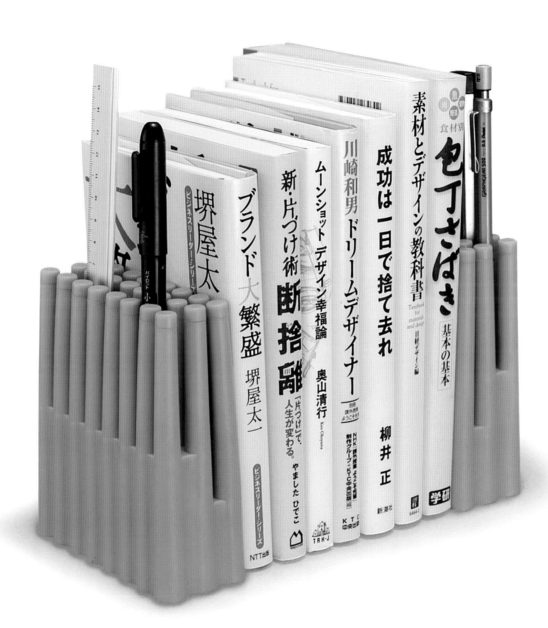

TATAMIZA
Kenya Hara // Hara Design Institute
2008 // Hida Sangyo

This sinuous loop of wood has the elegance of an antique bentwood chair but the function of conventional Japanese *zaisu*, or floor seating. One of six pieces created for the Japan Design Committee's 'Furniture for a Personal Use' project (see also *Step Step*, page 188), the legless *Tatamiza* chair is the product of the graphic designer-cum-design curator Kenya Hara. Household objects are not normally his field of work, but Hara applauded the Committee's initiative to pair designers with makers of wooden furniture; also, he was keen to make a seat for his own newly renovated, tatami-floored study.

What Hara envisioned was a chair that would not interfere with the room's sight lines nor take up too much space, but could act as 'an exterior skeleton', as he calls it, by providing plenty of support for the back. 'I was having lower back trouble so I had a very clear idea of where I needed back support', the designer explains. Although the realization of the *Tatamiza* took a whole year from planning to production, the chair's form emerged quickly.

Hara achieved his goal thanks to two curved bars: a rounded one to support the lower back, and a flattened one below that slides comfortably under the bottom. The two bars are connected, apparently seamlessly, by two acutely angled arm-like extensions. 'Typically, when you sit on a *zabuton* [floor cushion] your torso has to balance for support', says Hara; but with the *Tatamiza*, the pressure of body weight on the front bar sustains the seat's rear bar, which supports the back.

Achieving the precise shape of the seat took perseverance, and Hara welcomed the chance to work closely with his appointed manufacturer, Hida Sangyo, a Gifu Prefecture company that has been producing wooden furniture since 1920. Owing to the high level of skill required for the *Tatamiza*'s fabrication, each chair is made to order. Where possible, the manufacturer uses machines, such as presses to bend the oak bars. Tongue-and-groove joints hold the moulded pieces together, and a silky-smooth finish (achievable only by hand) blends the entire assembly into a single, fluid form.

Hara acknowledges that by making a few adjustments, the chair could be mass-produced, but that is not his aim. 'We have hit our goal already, so I am not in a rush to modify', he states.

084

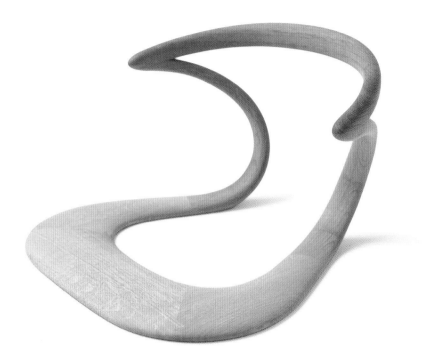

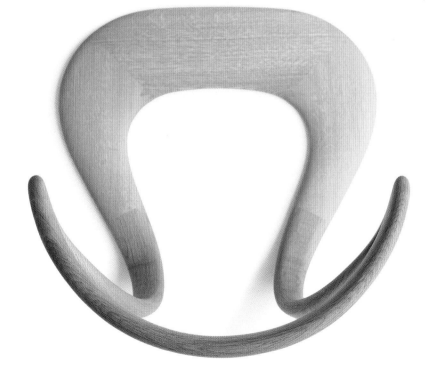

THIN BLACK LINES CHAIR
Oki Sato // Nendo
2010

At first glance, Nendo's *Thin Black Lines Chair* is a puzzling optical illusion. Composed of nineteen bent wires secured by an L-shaped metal frame, it uses a minimum of linear means to capture the essence of a three-dimensional object. The chair was created for the firm's first solo exhibition in the United Kingdom, at London's Saatchi Gallery in 2010. The show, titled *Thin Black Lines*, featured pieces made with black wire, and underscored Nendo's ability to turn the familiar into the unfamiliar and the mundane into the extraordinary (see also *Roll*, page 164).

The chair's design was preceded in 2009 by a series of shop displays in which Nendo used wire fixtures to display fashion designer Issey Miyake's new clothing line, '24' (a colourful collection of garments that takes its cue from Japan's ubiquitous convenience stores, where a wide range of ever-changing consumer goods is available round the clock). Inspired by standard shop fittings, Nendo used steel wire to create minimal furnishings that do not detract from the clothing.

In the *Thin Black Lines Chair*, instead of trying to make wire disappear, Nendo calls attention to it. The eight limited-edition chairs, which were constructed by a factory in Japan that specializes in fabricating small computer parts, are made of parallel wires painted matt black and positioned at a 45-degree angle to the frame of the chair. This arrangement of wires is a powerful visual device. It is capable of changing people's perception of the seat when viewed from different vantage points, and the abstract sequence of lines pares the chair down to its most elemental form. '[The lines] are condensed expressions of meaning, similar to Japanese calligraphy', says Nendo's founder, Oki Sato.

While the conspicuous absence of upholstery or of a solid seating surface does not compromise the chair's identity, it does have an effect on its functionality. Usability was not Nendo's primary goal, however: '[The chair] supports weight but it was not designed for comfort', he says mischievously.

085

TIGGY
Reiko Sudo // Nuno
2003

A smooth cotton cloth laced with wispy white threads, *Tiggy* defies convention but is rooted in tradition. Named after Mrs Tiggy-Winkle, a hedgehog created by the children's writer Beatrix Potter, the prickly fabric is the product of textile wizard Reiko Sudo. Deeply respectful of Japan's rich cultural heritage (see *Kibiso Sandals*, page 102) yet eager to embrace technological advance, Sudo has a remarkable gift for pairing unlikely elements and for borrowing methodology from different disciplines – often with astonishing results.

To a large extent these results stem from Sudo's hands-on creative process. 'I always design textiles with my fingers', she explains. Inspired by reinforced packaging tape remembered from childhood, she began *Tiggy* by swabbing small bundles of white cotton thread with *konnyaku* paste. (This sticky substance made from the root vegetable devil's tongue has been used for centuries to waterproof raincoats and umbrellas made of *washi* paper.) Next she sewed the hardened threads loosely into a piece of cloth and snipped each thread, transforming the smooth cotton into a fabric as tactile as the fur of a forest animal.

Unsurprisingly, the idea of a cloth with stiff strings poking out was not popular with the weavers at the mill in Yamanashi Prefecture, but the designer was unwilling to take 'no' for an answer. Instead she simplified the construction of the cloth by reducing the number of *konnyaku*-coated plies and increasing the woven length between their cut ends. 'Basically, I start with a goal, but the end product is almost always a little different', comments Sudo. 'For me, exact duplication is not important.'

Using punchcards, the factory programmed its loom to weave 400-m (just over 437-yd) batches of the new textile. But there was no high-tech way to cut the floating white threads, and this labour-intensive task had to be done by hand with a knife. Usually, loose, unwoven or cut threads designate the 'wrong' side of cloth, but for Sudo fabric does not have a front or a back. Nor does she consider her textiles' final use: her design work done, she leaves those decisions to the customer.

086

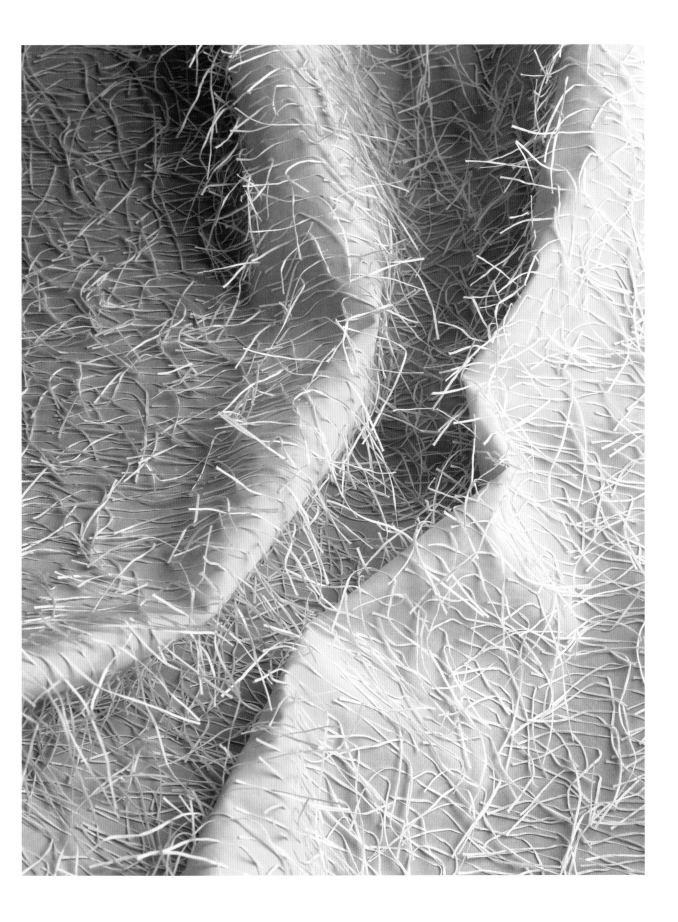

TILL
Mute
2010 // Duende

There are times when everyone wishes they had a temporary extra pair of hands. Straddling the line between object and furniture, the *Till* fits that bill. This simple steel stand, created by the Tokyo-based product-design company Mute, quietly does its job thanks to a horizontal bar on which to hang hooked items, such as umbrellas and shoe horns, and a flat tray for holding coins, keys and other pocket contents.

In common with many original objects, the *Till* was inspired by the wants of its designers, Keiji Ito and Takahiro Umino, who are intent on improving the cramped conditions of Japan's typically small homes. The duo identified a space-organizing need that was not being met and set about finding the perfect solution. Their first idea was for a rubber tray held against the wall by a single wooden rod, but a fellow designer's critique that the configuration was insecure and that people might trip over the pole led Ito and Umino back to the drawing board.

Six months later the designers introduced the prototype *Till* at the 2009 DesignTide Tokyo showcase, where it was spotted by Koji Nishiba of the design production company Duende. Although the *Till* would make an equally good tie rack or towel rail, Nishiba wanted to market it as an umbrella holder because, as he states, 'In Japan, it is better to introduce an item for one purpose only. If people have too many choices, they won't buy.' In addition, he recommended minor design adjustments in order to simplify the manufacture and packaging of the *Till*.

The stand is made entirely of steel by a local company specializing in commercial display fittings, and consists of three parts: a circular base; a rimless rectangular tray covered with a non-slip silicone pad; and a 13-mm-diameter (½ in.) vertical rod to connect the two. On the prototype, the connections were welded, but switching to screws enabled shipment in a flat box and quick assembly by the stand's owner. The rod is bent at 90 degrees in two places, so that it can both hold hanging items and support the tray. 'It can hold three or four umbrellas, but two look prettiest', says Umino knowingly.

087

TOASTER
Naoto Fukasawa
2007 // Plus Minus Zero

Created for browning a single slice of bread, Naoto Fukasawa's toaster is a charming version of the kitchen classic. It does not stray far from convention (a lever-operated slot for the bread sits in the centre, with an electric heating element on either side), but the toaster's cute shape and monochrome exterior set it apart from the pack. It measures just 22 cm (8⅝ in.) in length, and is only 8 cm (3⅛ in.) wide. While its diminutive size is right at home in Japan's often tiny domestic kitchens, the wide opening is perfect for a thick piece of white bread – a breakfast staple for a large segment of the population.

Although Portuguese traders may have introduced bread to Japan in the sixteenth century, the modern-day foodstuff did not really catch on until after the Second World War, when Western-style bakeries were on the rise nationwide. But, as in the case of many other things adopted from abroad by Japan, bread evolved to suit the local taste. White bread, as sold in Japanese supermarkets, convenience stores and a multitude of neighbourhood bakeries, has a very distinctive shape, being rectangular in section, not square. 'It is kind of an icon', explains Fukasawa. It is sold cut in various thicknesses, ranging from standard sandwich size to fat slabs usually eaten slathered with butter and jam.

It was from the familiar shape of a single slice of bread that Fukasawa took his first design cues, but convincing the manufacturer to make an appliance to this size took some effort. 'When we saw the first engineering drawing, we nearly gave up', the designer admits. The bulky, boxy outer shell offered protection from the build-up of heat inside, but was simply too large. Fortunately, by working closely with the factory, Fukasawa was able to whittle the case down to an acceptable size.

The toaster's petite proportions are not its only appeal; it has a sunny disposition, too: 'It's a happy, happy product', according to Fukasawa, who enjoys using it daily. The sight of browned bread popping up from the plain, smooth toaster delights the eye, while its enticing aroma gently awakens the palate.

088

TSUZUMI
Tomohiko Hirata // Ziba Tokyo
2012 // Stareast

Japan's population may be dropping, but pet ownership is on the rise. 'There are significantly more dogs and cats than there are children under fifteen years of age', reported PetFoodIndustry.com in an article titled 'Japanese Pet Population Increases, Petfood Ads Decrease' (March 2010). Pets, or rather their owners, are generating huge demand for a wide range of goods and services that extends well beyond food and basic medical care; stylish boutiques and swish grooming salons abound in Tokyo and other major cities. But all pet owners know that at some point they will have to part with their beloved animals: the life expectancy of dogs, for example, rarely exceeds fifteen years.

While Buddhism prescribes the rites relating to the death and mourning of human beings, there is no rule book for animals. As in the case of people, most pets are cremated, but their ashes are often mixed and interred in a group, so grieving owners who wish to save their pet's ashes have few options. 'They have to use an urn intended for a human being, and that's a little weird', says the product designer Tomohiko Hirata, who owns a toy poodle. The graphic-design concern Stareast,

which had identified a need, asked Hirata to make a receptacle for animal ashes that would be compatible with contemporary home decor.

Inspired by the form of the traditional *tsuzumi* drum, this elegant oval box consists of a flat stainless-steel lid and a teak base. They conceal a plastic container that can hold the ashes of any animal up to a mid-sized dog. The project designer Kayako Hirohashi considered a number of shapes, including that of a church, a pagoda and a classic dog bone, but eventually she settled on the *Tsuzumi*'s clean, abstract lines, the anonymity of which sits well even in a living room.

But behind this simplicity of design lies an arduous production process involving separate wood and steel fabricators. While the design phase lasted only a few weeks, it took months of product development and many prototypes to finalize the form of the urn, owing to the sensitivity of wood to humidity. Hirata had hoped to soften the appearance of the ashes in the urn with an interior coating of white lacquer, but in the end he had to accept a plastic insert. This has the benefit that it will preserve the ashes almost indefinitely.

089

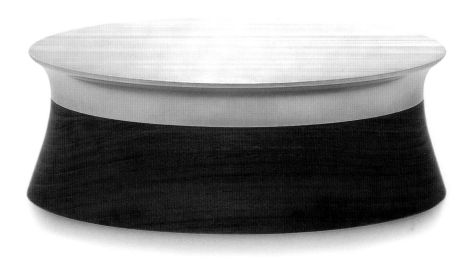

TUBELUMI
Hiroaki Watanabe // Plane
2009 // Nissho Telecom

The elegant *Tubelumi* desk lamp has a remarkable range of movement: it can extend all the way over an executive-sized desk or fold completely flat to half its length. The fixture consists of a weighted base that anchors a matt-finished metal tube hinged in three places. The lamp's exceptionally slim top tube – it is just 1.6 cm (⅝ in.) in diameter – holds the light source, a cold-cathode fluorescent lamp (CCFL; in such lighting, mercury vapour develops ultraviolet light, which in turn causes a fluorescent coating on the inside of the lamp to emit visible light).

CCFLs, which are economical and eco-friendly, attracted the attention of Nissho Telecom, a maker of electric appliances, and its president hired the industrial designer Hiroaki Watanabe to create a clever lamp design using the technology. After investigating a number of options, designer and client agreed that the three-hinged scheme was the best choice, but because the joints all swing 180 degrees, it was also the most difficult idea to realize, as only three factories in Japan have the capability to fabricate these complicated hinges – and none of them would consider making a small quantity for Nissho Telecom. In addition, CCFLs are hard to work with since they measure just 3 mm (⅛ in.) in diameter and break easily. Fortunately, Nissho Telecom's president tracked down a willing and able hinge-maker in Taiwan, where the hinges are commonly used by manufacturers of laptops. Taiwan is also a leading producer of CCFLs. That country was thus the logical place in which to assemble Watanabe's lamps.

Because it folds flat, the *Tubelumi* requires less packaging than other lamps, takes up less warehouse space and consumes less energy when transported from place to place. 'The president wanted to make a product that would be eco-friendly from factory to user', explains Watanabe. The *Tubelumi*'s CCFL light source lasts up to ten years and, unlike many alternatives, it emits cold light, which can translate directly into a reduction in air conditioning – a real saving in large offices loaded with worker bees.

090

TWELVE
Naoto Fukasawa
2005 // Seiko Instruments

Naoto Fukasawa started his career at Seiko Epson Corporation, a Japanese electronics giant known for its clocks. But when he was faced with the commission to create a wristwatch for the fashion designer Issey Miyake, he was determined to find a new, and simpler, idiom. His solution was a numberless timepiece that distils the iconic clock face to its very essence.

The face of Fukasawa's watch is articulated by a circular frame with an inner rim fashioned in the shape of a dodecagon (a plane figure with twelve straight sides and angles). In a clever merging of geometry and function, the twelve points of the inner rim demarcate the hours (hence the watch's name, *Twelve*). The watch's hands guide the eye towards the rim, but the mind must fill in the missing numbers.

For the time to be 'legible', both the hour and the minute hands had to have a strong presence; wide hands could achieve the desired visual effect, but extra weight ran the risk of interfering with the watch's delicate movement. Finding the right balance between these two considerations took many design iterations. Trading depth for width, Fukasawa designed hands that are exceptionally thin yet broad enough for the hour hand to hold the imprint of the brand name, Issey Miyake.

Depending on the model, the face is sealed with either clear or blue glass. This sits snugly beneath the faceted metal frame, which is integrated with the clock's stainless-steel body. Measuring close to 1 cm (⅜ in.) in depth, the chunky case slides on to the leather watchband and perches prominently on the wrist. 'The women's watch is very cute', asserts the designer with a smile.

In designing the *Twelve*, Fukasawa did not reinvent the wheel, nor was he the first designer to omit the numerals from a clock face. But the logical, twelve-sided frame is such a natural visual metaphor that the design of this watch seems likely to stand the test of time.

091

TWIGGY
Tomoko Azumi // T.N.A. Design Studio
2007 // Maxray

This delicate, fresh take on Japan's traditional paper lanterns was conceived in London, but born in Osaka. Commissioned and produced by Osaka-based Maxray, one of Japan's leading manufacturers of commercial lighting, the *Twiggy* lamp is the creation of the London-based designer Tomoko Azumi. Her enjoyment of forest walks in her adopted homeland inspired the fixture's organic form: a cylindrical lampshade of overlapping layers of a paper-like material cut into a pattern resembling bare winter branches (the 'twigs' behind the lamp's name), perched on a slender metal trunk.

The impetus for the genesis of the *Twiggy* lies with Maxray, which was keen to enter the retail market and asked Azumi to create lamps for domestic use. Following in the footsteps of generations of Japanese artisans, the designer looked to nature for ideas. 'I was thinking about how I could re-create the image of light coming through the layers and layers of twigs seen in the forest in winter', she explains.

This led Azumi to cut sheets of paper into five different types of twig shape, some of them quite figurative and some more abstract. Group by group, she scattered them randomly until she hit on an arrangement of sharply angled branches that yielded the right density and visual texture. She then recorded the pattern in a drawing measuring 1.6 m (more than 5 ft) in length – the actual length of the completed shade, since it wraps round the lighting element three times.

Given the intricacy and crisp edges of the pattern, Azumi envisioned laser-cutting the shades, but Maxray found a small local subcontractor able to complete the job with its economical and energy-saving die-cutting skills. Investigation was required in order to source the right material, too. After taking advice from a paper wholesaler, Azumi and her client selected a paper-like product made of polyethylene, a type of plastic. The material, commonly used for billboard posters, is both sturdy enough that the twigs will not snap off and fire retardant, so that it resists the inevitable build-up of heat from the bulb.

The lamp is packaged and sold tightly rolled up, accompanied by Maxray's electrical components, stainless-steel rod and base. After easy assembly by its owner, the *Twiggy* emits a soft glow reminiscent of the low winter sun.

092

TWO PIECE
Drill Design
2010 // Mizutori

Although traditional *geta* sandals are touted as beneficial to both the soles and the soul, they are a hard sell in contemporary Japan. Made of solid wood and cloth-covered straps, they are not particularly comfortable, nor are they easy to walk in, especially for anyone more used to trainers. Confident that it could improve the sandals so that they would appeal to customers from all walks of life, the *geta* manufacturer Mizutori asked Yoko Yasunishi and Yusuke Hayashi of Drill Design to do their bit to update the wooden classic.

Drill's first idea was to retool the sandal so that it would bend with the foot. 'When you walk in wooden shoes, the entire sole tilts up', explains Hayashi, but the foot wants to bend at the ball joint behind the toes. To ally shoe and foot, Drill proposed cutting the wooden sole into two pieces and inserting a strip of flexible foam rubber that bends with the foot, as well as adding a cushioning layer under the sole (opposite, bottom).

The designers had already worked with wood (see *Paper-Wood*, page 146), but in order to get up to speed on the mechanics of footwear they had to consult with Mizutori's experts at its headquarters in Shizuoka Prefecture, Japan's *geta*-making centre. They also tried on many *geta* and studied the movement of their own legs to get a feel for how they could improve the shoe. Armed with this empirical knowledge, Drill produced sketches and simple prototypes in their studio in Tokyo before developing the design in consultation with Mizutori.

The first two models to go on the market were the closed-toed Egg (opposite, top) and the open-toed Tunnel, both intended for indoor use and both unisex. The soles are cut from the traditional *geta* material, hinoki cypress grown in Shizuoka Prefecture, then are glued to the rubber and sealed with oil at Mizutori's factory. The black rubber contrasts sharply with the beige wood, visually calling attention to the shoe's unique construction. Thanks to a choice of three different colours of synthetic leather, the shoes offer fashion flexibility, since their simple styling goes equally well with jeans and kimono-like *yukata*.

093

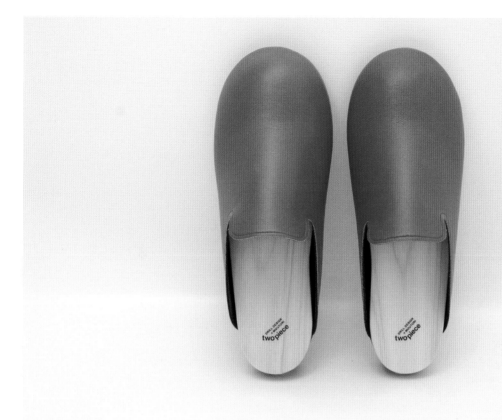

UMBRELLA TEA HOUSE
Kazuhiro Yajima // Kazuhiro Yajima Architect
2010 // Hiyoshiya Workshop

The *Umbrella Tea House* blends two of Japan's most treasured traditions, umbrella-making and the tea ceremony. A portable, tatami-floored room perfectly sized for the formal tea ceremony, it is enclosed in a cloth-covered bamboo frame structured in the manner of a large umbrella. Designed by the architect Kazuhiro Yajima and built by the Kyoto umbrella-maker Hiyoshiya Workshop, the mini-building is a true collaboration between craft and construction.

Japan's exquisite paper umbrellas, which Yajima likens to portable roofs, had fascinated him for some time, but the invitation to create a tea house for the World O-Cha (Tea) Festival in Shizuoka Prefecture in 2010 was his first chance to experiment with them at an architectural scale. Yajima envisioned quoting literally from the vocabulary of traditional umbrellas by building with bamboo and paper; translating these materials from one product to another, however, required some adjustments. He was aided in this process by Soshin Kimura, who acted as tea-ceremony consultant and creative supervisor.

As Yajima explains, 'Bamboo is strong, light and easy to work with, but it is breakable since the shrinkage rate between inside and out differs.' By borrowing the umbrella-maker's technique, Yajima circumvented this problem so that the bamboo did not crack. Although the 2.75-m-diameter (9 ft) tea house is supported by a single stalk of bamboo, this is not used as a central column. Instead, the umbrella-maker split the long pole lengthways into fifty strips; these were cut in two, then spliced and sewn back together to form hinged ribs that support both the wall and the roof. Finally, a milky-white non-woven fabric resembling traditional *washi* paper was lightly glued to the bamboo framework. 'The most difficult part was figuring out how to make doors', explains Yajima. He devised two entrances (a high one for the tea master and a low one for the guests), each consisting of hanging hinged panels.

When the festivities are over, the tea house is easily dismantled – with a fishing rod. A tug on the frame's concealed central ring leads the entire structure to fold up, umbrella-like, into a 3.6-m-long (just under 12 ft) bundle. The *Umbrella Tea House* may not fit comfortably inside a standard car, but the possible uses for a potentially portable building are endless.

094

WASARA
Shinichiro Ogata // Simplicity
2008

Wasara are surely among the most elegant disposable dishes on Earth. Made from readily renewable, biodegradable materials, they are comparatively good for the planet, too. But these plates and cups are so well crafted and delicately proportioned that it seems a shame to throw them out after just one use.

The word *wasara* translates as 'Japanese tableware', a fitting description of the dishes' origin. Created by the designer Shinichiro Ogata, the collection caters to Japanese cuisine, in which most meals, from top-tier *kaiseki* banquet down to *katei ryori* casual dining, consist of small portions of several different foods, each served in an appropriately shaped and sized dish. But the series is also suitable for Western food, as it includes a variety of round and rectangular plates, bowls, tumblers, and cups in various sizes for coffee, wine and *soba* noodles.

'Depending on the country, the way of using the dishes varies', explains Ogata. In Japan, people frequently pick up and hold up their dishes while eating, even when seated at the table, therefore the *Wasara* needed to be stiff and self-supporting. Several of the pieces have a built-in lip to make them easy to hold with one hand. And, in common with most Japanese tableware, all the dishes have a neat, rimless edge for easy chopstick use.

While the design of the dishes was achieved in one month, working out how to make them took three years. Ogata's quest led him to a manufacturer of car-engine parts that could fabricate the necessary metal moulds. In addition to forming the dishes' delicate shapes, the moulds impress on the surface of each piece a fine pattern that is intended to evoke the spirit of handcrafted *washi* paper. The collection is mass-produced, in off-white only, in China from a blend of bamboo, reed fibres and bagasse (a waste product from sugar-cane processing).

The material, which is left untreated, is strong – it can handle hot and cold food and drinks, and is oil- and water-resistant for up to ten hours – but silverware is its nemesis. Ogata is confident that he can overcome this weakness, and is expanding the series to include cutlery made of bamboo.

095

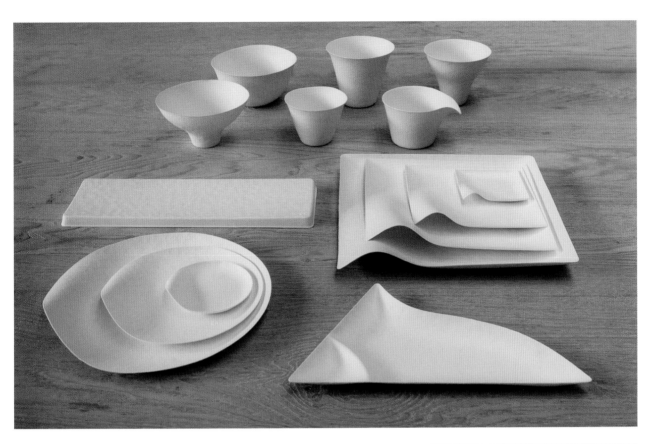

WHILL
Satoshi Sugie
2011

Riddled with narrow, crowded streets, Tokyo is not the most wheelchair-friendly place in the world. For people who are reliant on wheelchairs, just getting to a convenience store can be a colossal challenge, even though the shops are ubiquitous. Dismayed by the physical hardship and loss of freedom that many wheelchair users face daily, the designer Satoshi Sugie rallied a posse of fifteen young engineers, marketing specialists, industrial designers and other twentysomethings willing to explore uncharted territory. They pooled their talents to devise a swish prototype device, which they named *Whill*, that both offers better manoeuvrability and minimizes stigma.

Resembling a large pair of headphones, the *Whill* clamps on to a wheelchair's wheels and propels the vehicle by means of small battery-fed electric motors on either side; the streamlined, prow-like dashboard, which is made mostly of fibre-reinforced plastic, enables easy steering, even for individuals without the full use of their arms or hands. As in the case of a Segway 'personal transporter', a gentle push in the centre of the dashboard drives the chair forward, while pressure exerted on the *Whill*'s left or right side aims the chair in those respective directions. 'It's a new type of mobility', explains Sugie. It is also a dramatic visual improvement over the usual joystick-style wheelchair steering mechanism. '[*Whill*] has the aggressive image of driving', says the designer.

The development of the device began with field research at a physical-rehabilitation centre, where meetings with an engineer brought Sugie up to speed on wheelchair specifications. This was also an opportunity to interact with and observe potential *Whill* users. 'Most cannot imagine going outside easily on their own', reports the designer.

The team then began investigating where to position the motor for the best mobility and overall appearance. The two-pronged form was selected because dividing the motor in two improved weight distribution and enabled faster speeds; the *Whill* can reach 20 km/h (more than 12 mph), leaving conventional motorized chairs in the dust. A mechanized stand, coupled with hinges on either side of the *Whill*, enables the user to install the device with ease.

096

X-RAY
Tokujin Yoshioka
2010 // KDDI/iida

Japanese mobile phones are among the most sophisticated in the world. Their functions extend well beyond ordinary telecommunications – the phones double as televisions, train passes and body-fat calculators – and countless colour, shape and other aesthetic variations debut regularly. Against this challenging backdrop, the product designer Tokujin Yoshioka wanted to create a mobile phone the likes of which had never been seen before. 'The important thing for me is to take the audience beyond their imagination', he states. The *X-Ray*, rolled out in October 2010 by mobile-phone giant KDDI's iida brand (see also *Infobar A01*, page 92), does just that.

In common with many phones, the *X-Ray* is equipped with the latest features, such as a high-speed central processing unit to reduce call-processing time, and GSM standard to broaden coverage. Even its rectangular, flip-phone form does not stray very far from established norms. What distinguishes the *X-Ray* is the unique transparent skin that exposes the phone's inner workings, a complex but beautiful assembly of electronic elements.

Yoshioka worked from the inside out, configuring the phone's interior in collaboration with engineers, a first in mobile-phone design. 'We took it one problem at a time', he says. To improve the aesthetics of parts normally hidden from view, the designer reorganized the components and changed some of their colours, and specified the lettering used for labelling.

Yoshioka then moved on to the phone's exterior. The transparent shell, which is made of a durable polycarbonate infused with glass fibre and tinted a sophisticated shade of red, blue or black, practically melts away, while a band of LEDs zips across the phone's front, boldly announcing incoming calls, the current time and other information.

The design of the shell began with Yoshioka's computer-drawn sketch, which became the basis of a full-size mock-up made of clear acrylic. The designer sculpted this model as if he were crafting a work of art, chamfering its corners and paring it down wherever possible. 'I repeatedly tested it by actually holding it in my hand … a mere one-tenth of a millimetre difference could give the phone a different feel', he explains. The result of Yoshioka's fine-tuning is a phone that not only looks elegant but also fits well in the palm.

097

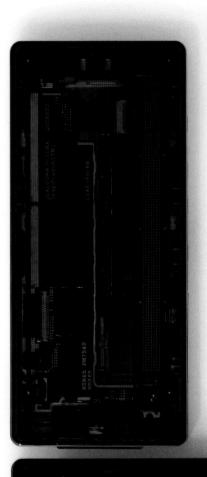

TOKUJIN YOSHIOKA

X-RAY TOKUJIN YC

YAMA
Mikiya Kobayashi // Mikiya Kobayashi Design
2011 // Takata Lemnos

Cheap, lightweight and cold to the touch, aluminium is not considered to be a precious metal. Yet Mikiya Kobayashi's salt and pepper dispensers (named after the Japanese word for 'mountain') deftly shake off that image, and the matching mounds of the silver-coloured metal sit as comfortably on the table as they do in the hand.

Although the shakers are made of metal, wood was at the root of Kobayashi's project. A group of household goods crafted by the Tokyo-based designer for a Hokkaido woodworking concern was seen by people at Takata Lemnos, a traditional metal-smithing company located in Toyama Prefecture. The firm then invited Kobayashi to create objects using its signature materials, brass and aluminium. The company's goal was not only to render metal more appealing but also to find contemporary applications for its traditional methods of making Buddhist ritual objects.

Kobayashi's starter collection for Takata Lemnos, called *Iki* (a combination of *imono*, or 'cast metal', and *ki*, meaning 'tool'), includes brass bottle openers and chopstick rests as well as candlesticks and an incense burner made of aluminium. 'The design concept was to make products that fit the hands', says Kobayashi. Since aluminium is lighter than brass, he had to weigh up which material to use for each product.

Brass felt too heavy for the *Yama* shakers, so Kobayashi chose aluminium instead. While the shakers' tops are polished, elsewhere Kobayashi preserved the naturally rough texture that results from the sand-casting process used in their fabrication. This method was employed both to reduce costs and as a reference to the traditional Japanese aesthetic of concealed beauty. 'It is like the collar on a kimono', explains the designer (everyone knows that a magnificent undergarment lies beneath the outer cover, but only a tiny bit shows). 'Leaving some parts [of the shakers] unpolished emphasizes the metal's beauty.' Because the function of the dispensers is to hold food seasoning, they are coated with an anti-corrosion sealant.

In common with ordinary shakers, the *Yama* pair are punctured on top with holes that sprinkle salt or pepper, and they feature a larger opening in the base through which to fill them. Although the shakers are functionally far from groundbreaking, their pleasing shape and tactility take the versatility of aluminium to new heights.

098

YU WA I
Yuki Tanaka // Architecture + Interior Design Issun
2011 // Arita Yusendo

No Japanese wedding is complete without gifts of money for the bridal couple. Each of these gifts is elegantly presented in a white envelope, sealed with a *mizuhiki* ceremonial paper cord that culminates in an exquisite knot appropriate to the occasion. Such knots are often used to adorn other celebratory gifts, too. Expanding on this idea, Yuki Tanaka created the *Yu Wa I* ('tying a knot in celebration'), a bottle-shaped bag made from a web of *mizuhiki*. Adorned with its festive square knots, the bottle-holder presents a gift of wine with panache and decorum.

The project began when Arita Yusendo, a *mizuhiki* manufacturing firm on the island of Shikoku, invited several young designers to create a contemporary product utilizing its traditional craft. The company was motivated by concern for the future of the *mizuhiki* industry, which is threatened by the increase of rope production in China and the decrease of skilled artisans in Japan.

Tanaka took up the firm's challenge. Her first step was to familiarize herself with the knots; she taught herself how to tie the complex forms by examining samples provided by Arita Yusendo. Once she had mastered the technique, Tanaka was able to play with composition and to manipulate variables, such as cord tension and number of plies. The square *awaji musubi* knot, which symbolizes a strong bond that lasts forever, became the building block of her bottle holder.

The loose-mesh container is made from 90-cm-long (roughly 35½ in.) strands of rope. Ribbon-like assemblies of eight cords apiece zigzag up the height of the bottle, coming together in a diamond-grid pattern in double-looped knots. 'If I used too few strands, the holder would be too weak, and with too many it would be too expensive', explains Tanaka. The knots culminate near the cork, where they gather the cords into a loop that serves as the bottle holder's handle.

Each cord consists of a coiled core of traditional *washi* paper wrapped in colourful silk-like rayon threads. Because of the thread's inherent slipperiness, Tanaka interwove the smooth strands with roughly textured ones laced with metallic polyester lamé. This enables the knots to retain their shape well, thus allowing the use of the *Yu Wa I* over and over again.

099

ZUTTO RICE COOKER
Fumie Shibata // Design Studio S
2004 // Zojirushi

The rice cooker is an appliance found in most Japanese kitchens. Electric hot pots that produce perfectly cooked grains every time, they serve up the staple of most Japanese meals. Yet, despite their omnipresence, rice cookers often look out of place. 'Most resemble space ships', laments the industrial designer Fumie Shibata. Knowing she could do better, she set her mind to creating a rice cooker that would be as much at home on a kitchen worktop as conventional pots and pans.

The *Zutto Rice Cooker* was the first of a trio of appliances designed by Shibata for the Zojirushi corporation, a leading manufacturer of electric housewares. The device's sleek oval form, which was inspired by the traditional bentwood box known as *magewappa*, is slightly smaller than the competition; as a result, it sits comfortably among other appliances in the kitchen. Nevertheless, it still yields a respectable ten portions of rice – the same as most standard cookers on the market.

The cooker's black-and-silver case has the timeless look of stainless steel, but in fact is made of plastic. Beneath this neutral skin lurk the machine's intricate inner workings. Thanks to its internal fuzzy logic (which follows 'if–then' rules), the *Zutto* can distinguish and prepare all manner of rice. Its microchip-controlled timer enables the owner to prepare the raw grain at night and wake up to fluffy white kernels for breakfast the next morning, and then to keep the leftovers warm all day.

Zojirushi periodically modifies the cooker's internal mechanism in line with technological advances, but its shape and exterior styling remain intentionally the same from year to year. This strategy contrasts sharply with the industry standard; in Japan household appliances are altered or updated every six to twelve months. 'The market constantly demands new things,' explains Shibata, 'but if a product is designed well, you should be able to sell and use it for a long time.' The *Zutto Rice Cooker* (named after the Japanese for 'always') is poised for a long shelf life.

100

DESIGNER PROFILES

& Design

Tokyo-based & Design was established in 2005 by Shigenori Ichimura, Tetsu Miyazawa, Maho Kusano and Keiichi Minamide. At the time they were all employed in the design divisions of large companies, but were keen to try their hands at designing a broader range of products. Their first collection, presented at the 100% Design Tokyo showcase in 2005, featured twelve household products that blurred the boundary between two- and three-dimensional design. Ichimura (born in Ibaraki Prefecture in 1972) and Miyazawa (born in Tokyo in 1972) now run the firm full-time, dividing their time between design commissions from manufacturers and self-generated projects.

www.anddesign.jp

Yukichi Anno // Anno Design Office

Anno (born in Tokyo in 1972) studied electrical engineering at Tokyo's Tamagawa University, but decided to become a product designer while working in Shizuoka Prefecture for model-kit-maker Bandai, and entered the master's course in industrial design at London's Central Saint Martins College of Arts and Design. On his return to Tokyo he worked at his father's product-design firm, Anno Associates, for four years before going freelance. He launched his own company in 2010.

www.anno-design.co.jp

Shigeru Aoki *see* Arnest

Arnest

Kitchen-goods specialist Arnest (founded by Kunio Suzuki in 1981) strives to make cooking implements that are fun to use and brighten up the room. The firm is located in Sanjo City, Niigata Prefecture, and has seventy employees, including thirteen designers. Shigeru Aoki (the designer of *Suspence*; born in 1971 in Niigata Prefecture) studied product design at Sendai's Tohoku Institute of Technology, then worked at a variety of companies, on designs ranging from satchels to sporting goods, before joining Arnest in 2006. Shunsuke Takahashi (the designer of *Round & Round*) was born in 1981, also locally, and educated at a technical school in Niigata; he joined

Arnest as an illustrator in 2005 and moved to product design in 2008.

www.ar-nest.co.jp

Yasuhiro Asano // Asano Design Studio

Asano (born in Saitama Prefecture in 1953) studied architecture at Tokyo's Kogakuin University, followed by packaging design at Kuwasawa Design School, and then launched his own firm. In 1988 he studied for a master's degree at Milan's Domus Academy. Today his studio is engaged in a wide range of graphic-, product- and space-design projects.

www1.nisiq.net/~asano/

Shin Azumi // A Studio

'I look at furniture the same way as designing a computer', says Shin Azumi (born in Kobe in 1965). He studied at Kyoto City University of Arts, then started his career in Tokyo at NEC Design Center, where he created a variety of electronic goods, including word processors, laptop computers and video-game consoles. He next studied for a master's in industrial design at London's Royal College of Art. After graduating in 1992 he was part of the London-based firm Azumi with Tomoko Azumi (below) before opening his own studio in 2005.

www.shinazumi.com

Tomoko Azumi // T.N.A. Design Studio

Tomoko Azumi (born in Hiroshima in 1966) has been intrigued by design since childhood. The daughter of an architect–structural engineer, she recalls summer holidays spent building houses from cardboard, chopsticks and toothpicks, and she went on to study architecture at Kyoto City University of Arts. After working for two years at a Tokyo architectural office, she took a master's degree in furniture design at London's Royal College of Art. She then opened a London office, Azumi, with Shin Azumi (above) before founding her own firm in 2005.

www.tnadesignstudio.co.uk

Masako Ban // Acrylic

Ban (born in Tokyo in 1963) began her design career after graduating from

college by working briefly at the avant-garde firm Shigeru Ban Architects, but was not fully convinced that she wanted to pursue the building arts. She went on to become a self-taught graphic designer, but switched to jewellery design and introduced her first acrylic collection in 2003. She opened her shop in Tokyo in 2005, named Acrylic after that material. From this tiny two-storey premises she shows her full line of jewellery as well as the handbags she designs with her sister, Tomoko Nakamura.

www.acrylic.jp

Color

'Everyone understands colour', says Akiko Shirasu, who in 2009 co-founded the Tokyo-based design firm Color with Noriyuki Shirasu and Toru Sato. The company creates a multifaceted range of products and furniture that incorporate the team's range of talents. Akiko Shirasu (born in Fukuoka in 1963) studied English at Nagasaki University of Foreign Studies and later worked as a copywriter. Noriyuki Shirasu (born in Tokyo in 1966) studied graphic design at Tokyo's Tama Art University before joining Mitsubishi Electric Corporation; stints at an advertising agency and a graphic-design firm followed. Toru Sato (born in Niigata Prefecture in 1968) studied product design at Tokyo's Nihon University before joining Mitsubishi Electric Corporation.

www.color-81.com

Cube Egg

Cube Egg was founded in Hyogo Prefecture in 2009 after Takayuki Sasaki (born in Toyama Prefecture in 1954) acquired an existing company that makes moulds for plastic goods. Having worked in the industry for years, he wanted to make household items for customers with an appetite for good design. Using his factory's technology, he collaborates with independent designers, makes the moulds for their plastic products and then uses local manufacturers to complete the production process. '"Made in China" is easy, but I am proud to manufacture in Japan', he says. The company's first product was the *Smart Bento* lunch-box set (2009).

www.cubeegg.com

D-Bros // Draft

D-Bros was launched in 1995 as the product-design division of Tokyo-based graphic design and advertising agency Draft (founded in 1978 by Satoru Miyata). Each year its graphic designers create several products that showcase amusement and whimsy, including stationery, calendars, glassware and other items that straddle the line between two and three dimensions.

www.d-bros.jp

Drill Design

Tokyo-based multidisciplinary design studio Drill Design was founded in 2000 by Yoko Yasunishi and Yusuke Hayashi. Yasunishi (born in Gifu Prefecture in 1976) studied sociology at Tokyo's Waseda University. Hayashi (born in Kanagawa Prefecture in 1975) studied economics at Tokyo's Gakushuin University. Both then studied design at ICS College of Arts, also in Tokyo. The two later worked at separate firms for a year before founding Drill Design, where they create new products and also engage in graphic- and interior-design projects.

www.drill-design.com

Flask

Flask was founded in 1999 by Naoko Matsumoto and Ryuichi Sato, former classmates at Tokyo's Kuwasawa Design School, but the association was short-lived. Matsumoto (born in Tokyo in 1974) knew from early childhood that she wanted to be an artist, and had insight into the design world thanks to a fashion-designer aunt. After her design studies she did odd jobs to earn a living, but soon launched Flask with Sato (born in Fukushima Prefecture in 1976). Although their products garnered immediate attention, the designers dissolved their company after only a few years.

Shigeki Fujishiro // Shigeki Fujishiro Design

Fujishiro (born in Tokyo in 1974) studied economics at Tokyo's Wako University, then went to study English in Berkeley, California, where his appreciation of the city's historical buildings sparked an interest in architecture. On returning to Tokyo he entered the space-design programme at Kuwasawa Design School, after which he worked as a furniture designer for the interiors company Idee. 'I feel that furniture is small architecture', he explains. Fujishiro left Idee in 2005 and launched his own practice soon afterwards.

www.shigekifujishiro.com

Naoto Fukasawa

Fukasawa (born in Yamanashi Prefecture in 1956) is engaged in a wide range of design projects, including mobile phones, personal computing products, electronics, household goods, furniture and interiors. His products are owned by museums around the world. In addition to collaborating with Japanese manufacturers, he works regularly with brands throughout Europe and Asia. In addition, he is one of the directors of the design gallery 21_21 Design Sight in Tokyo, is a member of the design advisory board for the Muji label, and has chaired Japan's Good Design Award jury. He is the author of several books on design, including *The Outline* (2009) and the monograph *Naoto Fukasawa* (2007). He is the recipient of numerous international awards, and was granted the title Honorary Royal Designer for Industry by Britain's RSA (Royal Society for the encouragement of Arts, Manufactures and Commerce).

www.naotofukasawa.com

Furnish

Tokyo-based self-production design firm Furnish was founded in 2005 by Satoshi Yoshikawa and Bungo Komuro. Yoshikawa (born in Tokyo in 1974) was working for a boutique eyewear company when he decided to study design; he entered Tokyo's Aoyama Fashion College, where he met Komuro (born in Kanagawa Prefecture in 1973). When they founded Furnish they intended to design furniture, but they soon switched to creating small pieces that they could make on their own. Marie Hontoku (born in Tokyo in 1987), who studied product design at Tokyo Polytechnic University, is a recent addition to the firm.

www.furnish.jp

Kenya Hara // Hara Design Institute

Hara (born in Okayama Prefecture in 1958) trained as a graphic designer but has emerged as one of Japan's leading design theoreticians and curators. Since 2002 he has been a member of Muji's design advisory board and has acted as the company's art director. A prolific writer, he also continues to create commercial products and signage for many of Japan's leading brands.

www.ndc.co.jp/hara/about/en

Noriko Hashida // Noriko Hashida Design

Hashida (born in Aichi Prefecture in 1964) envisioned becoming a graphic designer but realized after enrolling at the design department of Tokyo National University of Fine Arts and Music (now Tokyo University of the Arts) that she did not want to limit herself to two dimensions, and she switched to the industrial design course. 'Designing 3D, daily-life objects was more interesting to me', she explains. Many of her classmates wanted to pursue careers in automotive or electronics design, but Hashida chose sanitaryware and joined the plumbing-fixture giant Toto. She left the company in 2009 to launch her own practice.

http://hashidadesign.com

Takanori Hayakawa // C.H.O. Design

Hayakawa (born in Aichi Prefecture in 1966) decided to become a designer during high school. Because he liked painting he thought he would pursue graphics, but instead he studied product design at Kanazawa College of Art. He then joined the design department at the INAX corporation, where he worked on a variety of plumbing and kitchen fixtures, and eventually moved to D'Code, a product-design concern in Tokyo that specializes in electronics. In 2008 he established his own practice.

www.chodesign.jp

Atsuhiro Hayashi

Hayashi (born in Kyoto in 1967) studied design at Kyoto Seika University, then joined a Kyoto-based printing company, where he worked on package design for three years. Next he joined a firm that specializes in package design for cameras and other products requiring intricate wrapping and presentation. Motivated by the feeling that 'the consumer wants the product, not its packaging', he moved to a design studio in Osaka, where he created kitchenware, including measuring spoons, for fourteen years. He went freelance in 2009.

http://a-hayashi.com

Naoki Hirakoso // Hirakoso Design

Hirakoso (born in Tokyo in 1974) had his heart set on going to art school, but instead entered the design department at the Tokyo National University of Fine Arts and Music (now Tokyo University of the Arts). 'I realized that individuals buy paintings to decorate their homes,' he says, 'but I wanted to do something that would reach lots of people.' After graduating he worked for the Conran Shop as a display designer, then, to familiarize himself further with Western lifestyles and furnishings, spent two years in Milan. In 2006 he returned to Tokyo and started his firm.

www.hirakoso.jp

Tomohiko Hirata // Ziba Tokyo

Hirata (born in Kanagawa Prefecture in 1957) first became interested in design as a high-school student after reading a book about jewellery design belonging to his father, who had a jewellery shop. He studied industrial design at Nagakute city's Aichi Prefectural University of Fine Arts and Music, then worked for Canon in Tokyo for six years before moving to the Bridgestone corporation. In 1994 he joined Ziba Design in Portland, Oregon, but two years later returned to Tokyo, where he became the design manager at the design promotion company Axis. He launched Ziba Tokyo in 2006.

www.ziba-tokyo.com

Keigo Honda // Honda Keigo Design

Honda (born in Fukuoka Prefecture in 1974) grew up with design in the air: his grandmother had a made-to-order clothing business, and his family home was full of traditional furniture and handicrafts. At Tokyo Zokei University he

intended to study automotive design but switched his focus to furniture. He then worked at outdoor-gear-maker Snow Peak in Niigata Prefecture, which combined his design education with his passion for outdoor sports and mountain climbing. After ten years of designing tents, camping chairs and outdoor cookware he returned to Tokyo, where he now teaches at Kuwasawa Design School and works as a freelance designer.

Takuya Hoshiko // Design Office FrontNine

Hoshiko (born in Kumamoto City in 1974) grew up wanting to study art, but a change of heart led him to a job at a furniture company, where he crafted chairs for six years before studying interior design at Tokyo's Kuwasawa Design School. He then worked for five years at a graphic-design firm, and then for two years in the design department of a general merchandise company. He opened his own office in 2006, from where, capitalizing on his rich and varied background, he works in various media, including graphic and product design.

www.dof9.com

Hisae Igarashi // Igarashi Design Studio

Igarashi (born in Tokyo in 1964) became interested in interior and 3D design while at school. She studied interior design at Tokyo's Kuwasawa Design School, then entered Shiro Kuramata Design Office, where she worked for more than five years on a variety of interiors, including restaurants and shops, as well as furniture. She established her own studio in 1991. Today she and her staff of five are engaged mostly in interior and shop design, but also undertake numerous product-design projects.

www.igarashidesign.jp

Toyo Ito // Toyo Ito & Associates, Architects

Ito (born in Seoul, South Korea, in 1941) studied architecture at the University of Tokyo, then worked for Kiyonori Kikutake Architects for four years before opening his own company, Urban Robot (Urbot), in Tokyo in 1971; the firm was renamed Toyo Ito & Associates, Architects in 1979. His

architectural works include Sendai Mediatheque (2001), Tod's Omotesando Building (2004) and Tama Art University Library (2007). He is also a prolific product designer, and has created light fixtures for Yamagiwa, door handles for Olivari and tableware for Alessi.

www.toyo-ito.co.jp

Genta Kanayama // Genta Design

Kanayama (born in Tokyo in 1964) was exposed to the design world through his father, a graphic designer. As a secondary-school pupil he had dreamed of creating cars, but he studied product design at Tokyo's Kuwasawa Design School. He then moved to Osaka and spent six years working for IDK Design Laboratory, but returned to Tokyo in 1992 to begin his solo career. His first product was a computer table for the Kokuyo company. He established Genta Design with his wife, Chie Kanayama, in 2004.

www.gentadesign.com

Hideo Kanbara // Barakan Design

Kanbara (born in Hiroshima in 1978) came to design through car repair; the son of a garage owner, he remembers his father constantly taking things apart and putting them back together. Having absorbed that knowledge, he studied product design at Tokyo Zokei University. He then spent three years with the plumbing-products manufacturer Toto, followed by five at the advertising agency Dentsu, where he honed his art-direction and graphic skills. He launched his own practice in 2010, but also collaborates with academics as a special researcher at the University of Tokyo's Research Center for Advanced Science and Technology.

www.barakan.jp

Motomi Kawakami // Kawakami Design Room

Kawakami (born in Hyogo Prefecture in 1940) studied industrial design at the Tokyo National University of Fine Arts and Music (now Tokyo University of the Arts), then worked in Milan for the architect Angelo Mangiarotti for several years. He returned to Tokyo in 1971 and set up his own design firm. During the course of his career he has worked in a wide range of design fields, including furniture, household goods and interiors; he was also involved in the landscape design around Yokohama's Tsurumi Tsubasa Bridge (1994).

www.motomi-kawakami.jp

Toshiyuki Kita // IDK Design Laboratory

Kita (born in Osaka in 1942) studied at his home town's Naniwa Design College, then worked for several years at a local aluminium factory developing new product designs. In 1967 he started his practice in Osaka. His numerous collaborations with European fabricators began after a trip to Italy in 1969, during which he met Cesare Cassina, the president of a famous Italian furniture company. Now dividing his time between studios in Milan and Osaka, he produces a wide range of goods, including many that champion Japan's traditional craft culture.

www.toshiyukikita.com

Mikiya Kobayashi // Mikiya Kobayashi Design

Kobayashi (born in Tokyo in 1981) practised calligraphy as a child with his grandmother, a pivotal experience that developed his sense of space. He began thinking seriously about becoming a designer as a teenager, after reading a magazine article about the history of chairs, and studied interior design at Tokyo's Musashino Art University. He later worked for the commercial interiors firm Field Four Design Office for a year before starting his own practice in 2006. In 2011 he opened the design-goods shop Taiyou no Shita ('Under the Sun') in Tokyo.

www.mikiyakobayashi.com

Masayuki Kurakata // Monos

Kurakata (born in Tokyo in 1958) first became interested in design in secondary school after realizing that few objects both look good and function well. After studying industrial design at Tokyo Zokei University, he worked for a car company before teaming up with a group of colleagues to form an independent firm called INDECS, then a few years later left to travel the world. After returning

to Japan, Kurakata opened his own design office, Seltz, in 1991, with his wife, Yasuko Kurakata; he formed the design production company Monos with Shuta Kashiwagi in 2006.

www.monos.co.jp

Jin Kuramoto // Jin Kuramoto Studio

Kuramoto (born on Awaji island in 1976) grew up on the island surrounded by nature (Awaji was later the epicentre of Japan's Great Hanshin Earthquake of 1995), but left to study design at Kanazawa College of Art. He then joined the electronics company NEC, for which he worked both in Tokyo and in the Beijing office on the design of mobile phones and other electronic goods. While employed there he began taking on freelance design work with a friend, and went independent in 2008.

www.jinkuramoto.com

Marna

Tokyo-based housewares manufacturer Marna was founded in 1872 in Niigata Prefecture by Toramatsu Nagoya as a maker of brushes for cleaning and painting, and moved to its current site alongside Tokyo's Sumida River in 1905. The facility was destroyed twice, first by the Great Kanto Earthquake in 1923 and again by bombs during the Second World War, prompting the construction of a separate, new factory in Ibaraki Prefecture. The company, which remains under the control of the Nagoya family, now produces a wide range of household goods, most of them designed in-house.

www.marna-inc.co.jp

MisoSoupDesign

Architecture firm MisoSoupDesign was established by Daisuke Nagatomo and Minnie Jan in New York in 2004, and relocated to Tokyo in 2010. Nagatomo (born in Miyazaki Prefecture in 1977) studied at Tokyo's Meiji University and Columbia University in New York, then worked at Ten Arquitectos and Design Office for Research and Architecture, both in New York. Jan (born in Taiwan in 1979) studied architecture at the University of Southern California and

Columbia University, then worked for the architecture firm FXFOWLE in New York. MisoSoupDesign pursues both architectural and furniture design.

www.misosoupdesign.com

Sotaro Miyagi // Miyagi Design Office

Miyagi (born in Tokyo in 1951) had an interest in car design from a young age, but after sight problems prevented him from getting a driving licence he switched directions and turned to product design instead. After graduating from Chiba University he entered the Tokyo design and marketing firm Hamano Institute. He left the company in 1988 to launch his own practice. Over the years Miyagi undertook a wide range of design projects, including graphics, products, packaging, interiors and corporate logos. He died in 2011.

www.kt.rim.or.jp/~miyagi

Naori Miyazaki

Miyazaki (born in Gunma Prefecture in 1977) felt the pull of design from the age of fifteen. Fascinated by Japan's famous high-speed 'bullet trains' and other vehicles, he dreamed of designing transportation devices, but ultimately turned his attention to household goods instead. After studying product design at Tokyo's Tama Art University, he worked for a furniture-maker for several years before joining Idea International. A retailer and producer of interior goods and appliances founded in 1995, the firm both employs in-house designers and commissions freelancers to develop new products.

www.idea-in.com

Daisuke Motogi // Daisuke Motogi Architecture

Motogi (born in Saitama Prefecture in 1981) first became interested in design as a secondary-school pupil through a fascination with record sleeves, but studied architecture at Tokyo's Musashino Art University. 'Designing large-scale works appealed to me', he explains. He then joined the Tokyo firm Sschemata Design, where he worked on architectural, interior and product design for six years. In 2010 he launched his own firm, which engages in a variety of interior- and shop-design projects.

www.dskmtg.com

Chiaki Murata // Metaphys

Murata (born in Tottori Prefecture in 1959) studied applied physics at Osaka City University, and started his design career at Sanyo Electric in 1982. He left in 1986 and launched Hers Experimental Design Laboratory, the parent company of his design firm Metaphys, which works with manufacturers to produce a wide range of household and personal goods.

www.metaphys.jp

Mute

Tokyo-based product-design company Mute was founded in 2008 by Keiji Ito (born in 1983 in Shimane Prefecture) and Takahiro Umino (born in 1981 in Tokyo), graduates of the product-design course at Tokyo's Kuwasawa Design School and former colleagues at a space- and exhibition-design company. Their firm's name, Mute, reflects their philosophy that good design should not shout out but blend quietly with its surroundings. *Till* is Mute's first product to go into mass production, but the duo also market self-produced goods directly on the internet.

www.mu-te.com

Satoshi Nakagawa // Tripod Design

'My first career was teaching children', explains Tokyo-based Nakagawa (born in Ibaraki Prefecture in 1953), who studied design education at Chiba University. His second career was at Motorola in Japan and Chicago for ten years. He then founded his own design firm, Environmental Design Studio, in 1987 (renamed Tripod Design in 2000). In the 1990s he began research into 'universal design', his current passion and the focus of his practice. 'We have been focusing on the "average". But who is that?' he asks. 'I think good design should be universal.'

www.tripoddesign.com

Naruse Inokuma Architects

Yuri Naruse (born in Aichi Prefecture in 1979) knew from a young age that she wanted to do something creative, but it was not until she entered the University of Tokyo that she decided on architecture. After undergraduate studies, a master's degree and a doctorate, in 2005 she launched her own practice. Two years later she teamed up with Jun Inokuma (born in Kanagawa Prefecture in 1977), who first studied urban design at the University of Tokyo but switched to architecture. He worked for Chiba Manabu Architects for two years before joining Naruse.

www.narukuma.com

Nikko

China company Nikko was founded in the city of Kanazawa in 1908 as Nihon Koshitsu Toki, a producer of semi-porcelain dinnerware, a significant portion of which was exported overseas. In 1961 the company relocated its head office and main factory to neighbouring Ishikawa Prefecture, and this modernization coincided with the growth in the local market for Western tableware that began in the post-war period. The company now produces dishes in shapes and sizes that cater to Western and Japanese cuisines alike, for both commercial and home use, and its china is manufactured at factories in Japan, Malaysia and Thailand.

www.nikkoceramics.com

Nosigner

Tokyo-based design firm Nosigner was founded in 2006; its broad capabilities include product and graphic design as well as architecture and art direction. 'We have no boundaries', explains Eisuke Tachikawa, a representative of Nosigner. Preferring to remain anonymous, the group goes by an invented name that refers to the invisible relationships that its members seek to develop between humans and their environment. The group is also committed to using its members' skills to better society; within hours of the Great East Japan Earthquake in March 2011, for example, it had set up a website that enabled people around the world to post survival skills that might be useful to those in need.

www.nosigner.com

Shinichiro Ogata // Simplicity

Ogata (born in Nagasaki in 1969) trained as a designer, then began his career developing commercial spaces; he launched his own company in 1998. Instead of marketing his services to others, he became his own client by opening a restaurant featuring Japanese cuisine. Unable to procure tableware to his liking, he created his own. Today he collaborates with ceramicists, pewter smiths, confectioners and other artisans from various parts of Japan, using their expertise to make everyday goods and housewares that evoke the spirit of traditional Japan but are relevant to contemporary life.

www.simplicity.co.jp

Kouichi Okamoto // Kyouei Design

Okamoto (born in Shizuoka City in 1970) worked abroad as a sound producer for Dutch and British techno-music labels for ten years. During this time, he encountered Dutch design and also acquired a new appreciation of Japanese culture. On returning home he began design work of his own. His first project was *Balloon Lamp* (2005). To raise money for supplies and to learn the tricks of the trade, he held a variety of part-time jobs, including at his father's company, a maker of car-headlight parts. In 2006 he opened his studio, the name of which is borrowed from his father's company.

www.kyouei-ltd.co.jp

Gaku Otomo // Stagio

Otomo (born in Tokyo in 1978) grew up in Saitama Prefecture, but returned to Tokyo to study design at the Vantan Design Institute. He then picked up a wide range of practical skills through working at a series of different firms, including a furniture company, an interior-design firm and a printing company. After a two-month interlude travelling across Europe by bus, he returned to Tokyo and freelance design work. He launched Gakudesign in 2008. Now renamed Stagio, the firm today undertakes a variety of graphic- and product-design work as well as art-direction projects.

http://stagio.co.jp

Pinto

The mostly virtual design partnership (named after a word meaning 'focus') was formed in 2008 by Takanori Hikima and Masayoshi Suzuki, who met at Nihon University's College of Art in Tokyo, where they both studied industrial design. A basketball player at secondary school, Hikima (born in Saitama Prefecture in 1983) had dreamed of designing trainers, whereas Suzuki (born in Chiba Prefecture in 1982) had hoped to design chairs. They both work as in-house designers, at an electronics company and an office-furniture manufacturer respectively, but by night (and at the weekends) they collaborate on Pinto's annual themed collection of household goods.

www.pinto-design.jp

Toshihiko Sakai // Sakai Design Associate

Sakai (born in Kochi Prefecture in 1964) decided to become a product designer when in secondary school, and, as a motorcycle enthusiast, he hoped to create better bikes by studying design. Because he felt that motorbike design was already 'cool' when he graduated from Tokyo Zokei University in 1987, and therefore did not need his design capability, he instead entered a small firm that created electric musical instruments. He then spent a year surfing in Australia, before founding his own business in 1992. As both a designer and a design producer he creates a wide range of products, including 'advanced design' ideas for electronics firms, but has yet to design a motorbike.

www.sakaidesign.com

Nobuhiro Sato // Pull + Push Products

Nobuhiro Sato (born in Kanagawa Prefecture in 1977) graduated from architecture studies at Kyoto Seika University in 1999. He chose not to pursue a career in building construction, and instead entered a small Kyoto company that manufactures display fixtures and decorative ornaments. He began his independent design work in his spare time, making incense pots and planters from concrete. In 2002 he went independent and established his own firm. He makes all his products by hand from readily available raw materials, and sells them online, at exhibitions and at his shop in Kyoto, Comado.

www.pull-push.com

Oki Sato // Nendo

Oki Sato (born in Toronto in 1977) lived in Canada until the age of ten, when his family relocated to Japan. He studied architecture at Tokyo's Waseda University, then immediately launched his own practice. The firm's first project was to transform an old house near Tokyo's Shingawa station into a French restaurant using nothing but cloth, since the budget was very low. A visit to the Milan Furniture Fair convinced Sato to broaden the scope of his work. Today the firm's range includes architecture, interiors and a wide array of products.

www.nendo.jp

Taku Satoh // Taku Satoh Design Office

As a child, when he was not exploring urban wildlife in the fields near his Tokyo home, Satoh (born in 1955 in Tokyo) played with compasses and modelling clay. The son of a designer and nephew of an engine manufacturer, he developed an early appreciation for well-made machinery, but his secondary-school interest in record-sleeve design led him to study design at Tokyo National University of the Fine Arts and Music (now Tokyo University of the Arts). He then worked for the advertising agency Dentsu for a few years before opening his own design practice. He is also a director of Tokyo's 21_21 Design Sight gallery.

www.tsdo.jp

Fumie Shibata // Design Studio S

Shibata (born in Yamanashi Prefecture in 1965) knew from a young age that she wanted a job where she would be able to make things. The daughter of textile manufacturers in a small city in Yamanashi Prefecture, she considered a career in fabric but studied industrial design at Tokyo's Musashino Art University. She then worked for three years as an in-house designer at Toshiba Design Center, where she created small electrical appliances, such as hairdryers and shavers. In 1994 she started her own studio and began creating a wide range of household and electronic goods. More recently she has broadened her scope to include interior design, such as the sleeping-pod hotel 9h.

www.design-ss.com

Takumi Shimamura // Qurz

Shimamura (born in Kochi Prefecture in 1963) grew up surrounded by creative people: his grandfather crafted wooden shoes and his mother made kimonos. He knew from childhood that he wanted to be an artist, but shifted to design when he entered Tokyo Zokei University. 'At first I was interested in small things,' he says, 'but I liked big things, too.' In order to do both, he went into automotive design and joined Fuji Heavy Industries, working initially at its Subaru brand and then at its subsidiary design company Tug International. He opened his own firm in 2005.

www.t-shima.com

Reiko Sudo // Nuno

Sudo (born in Ibaraki Prefecture in 1953) grew up in the countryside, surrounded by a large extended family, and every year itinerant cloth merchants visited her homestead. 'All those bolts of silk laid out on the tatami mats were such a lovely sight', she says. 'That was my first motivation to become a textile designer.' A graduate of Tokyo's Musashino Art University, she launched her career weaving tapestries for architectural installations and designing print patterns for a large textile manufacturer. In 1982 she met Junichi Arai, a textile designer then employed by fashion label Issey Miyake, and joined him in developing the innovative fabric company Nuno. In 1987 Arai left the company and Sudo began running the business. Today Nuno has more than 2000 textiles in production.

www.nuno.com

Satoshi Sugie

Sugie (born in Shizuoka Prefecture in 1982) studied business administration at Kyoto's Ritsumeikan University. He then studied drawing and entered the design department of Nissan Motors, working primarily on exterior car design. He left the company in 2009 to found Smile Park, an organization devoted to design projects inspired by local communities around the globe. He is also known by the moniker sugiX, which combines the designer's family name with the mathematical symbol 'x'.

www.whill.jp

Eiji Sumi // DesignWater

Sumi (born in Gifu Prefecture in 1973) studied design at secondary school, after which he worked for a clothing company and then apprenticed himself to a furniture-maker in Hida Takayama, a Gifu town famous for its woodworking. This led him to study woodwork at a local technical college, and later to start his own firm in Gifu City. He now engages in a wide range of design work, including furniture, product and interior design. 'Just like water, I try to design without being tied to any genre or concept', he says.

www.designwater.net

Shinichi Sumikawa // Sumikawa Design

Sumikawa (born in Tokyo in 1962) studied industrial design at Chiba University, then joined the Sony corporation as a product designer. Working both in Japan and in the United States, he designed a range of goods for the electronics giant, including Walkmans, radios, headphones and television sets. He went solo in 1992 and established Sumikawa Design in Tokyo. While championing the importance of function in consumer products, he aims to create objects that also add a little levity to daily life.

www001.upp.so-net.ne.jp/sumikawa

Takeo Sunami // TSDesign

Since he liked working with his hands, Sunami (born in Kagawa Prefecture in 1973) knew from a young age that he wanted to be a designer. He studied product design at Chiba Institute of Technology, then worked for five years as a designer at a bed manufacturer in Tokyo. Inspired by the success of his scheme for a space-saving bed that stores away vertically, he went

independent in 2002, and has since been engaged in a wide variety of projects, including toys, furniture and electronics.

www.tsdesign.jp

Keita Suzuki // Product Design Center

Keita Suzuki (born in Aichi Prefecture in 1982) was first exposed to design at the age of fourteen when he encountered a chair made by Charles and Ray Eames. 'I was amazed that such a beautiful chair existed', he marvels. He went on to study product design at Tokyo's Tama Art University. He came into contact with Sugahara Glassworks, fabricator of his *Fujiyama Glass*, during his student days, when the company made a Martini glass for him that he entered in a competition hosted by the gin-maker Bombay Sapphire. Following in-house stints at design firms, he launched his own company, Product Design Center, in 2012.

www.productdesigncenter.jp

Masaru Suzuki // Ottaipinu

Masaru Suzuki (born in Chiba Prefecture in 1968) planned to study graphic design when he entered Tokyo's Tama Art University, but Hiroshi Awatsuji, a well-known textile designer and professor at the university, convinced him to change courses. After receiving his degree Suzuki worked for Awatsuji for four years, learning the ropes of interior and printed-fabric design. In 1996 Suzuki opened his own studio, Unpiatto, named after the Italian for 'one plate' in a reference to his ceramicist wife's work. Ottaipinu is one of Suzuki's signature textile brands.

www.unpiatto.com

Sachiko Suzuki // Schatje Design

Sachiko Suzuki (born in Tokyo in 1977) attended an art secondary school before matriculating at Tokyo's Musashino Art University, where she studied sculpture. Keen to pursue a career in design, she went to The Netherlands to study 3D design at Utrecht School of the Arts, then studied product design at the Design Academy Eindhoven. She worked for the Setagaya Monozukuri Gakko, a former Tokyo middle school transformed

into studio space for artists and designers, before launching her self-production firm in 2010.

www.schatje-d.com

Shunsuke Takahashi *see* Arnest

Takano

The company was founded in 1941 by Tadayoshi Takano, initially as a maker of precision springs; over the years it has expanded into other areas of manufacturing, including office furniture, advanced electronic equipment and health-care items, such as wheelchairs, and it now has bases throughout the country and overseas. The ageing of Japan's population leads the company to envision that its health-care department will grow.

www.takano-net.co.jp

Yuki Tanaka // Architecture + Interior Design Issun

Tanaka (born in Kyoto in 1969) grew up in Osaka just a stone's throw from the architect Tadao Ando's Rokko Housing project (1983 and 1993). Under the spell of this influential building complex, she studied architecture at Tokyo's Musashino Art University. She worked at Studio 80, the interior-design firm spearheaded by the renowned Shigeru Uchida, for five years, then travelled and worked in Europe for a year. On returning to Tokyo, she worked freelance before opening her own office.

www.yukitanaka.biz

Naoki Terada // Teradadesign Architects

Terada (born in Osaka in 1967) was raised in the Tokyo suburb of Tachikawa. He was acquainted with design from a young age, as his father is a graphic designer, but his keen interest in making models revealed an early leaning towards three-dimensional objects. As a secondary-school pupil he decided to pursue a career in architecture, since he was also interested in mathematics and physics. After studying engineering at Meiji University in Tokyo, he worked in Australia and Italy before enrolling in the master's programme at the Architectural Association School of Architecture,

London. He then worked freelance until he founded his Tokyo-based practice, Teradadesign Architects, in 2003.

www.teradadesign.com

Norihiko Terayama // Studio Note

Terayama (born in Tochigi Prefecture in 1977) studied architecture at Tokyo's Chuo College of Technology, and then product design at Kanazawa International Design Institute. He furthered his design education in The Netherlands at the Design Academy Eindhoven, followed by a year interning at Studio Richard Hutten, then engaged in a joint venture with the architecture firm MVRDV. He returned to Tokyo in 2006 and soon launched Studio Note – a name that combines the first syllables of his names but also references the first note or sketch that begins every design project.

www.studio-note.com

Tonerico

Tokyo-based interior- and product-design firm Tonerico was founded in 2002 as a three-person partnership. Hiroshi Yoneya (born in Osaka in 1968) studied industrial design at Tokyo's Musashino Art University, then worked for designer Shigeru Uchida's Studio80. Ken Kimizuka (born in Kanagawa Prefecture in 1973) studied architecture, also at Musashino Art University, and also worked at Studio 80. Yumi Masuko (born in Tokyo in 1967) studied at Tokyo's Joshibi University of Art and Design and worked as a design producer. The threesome are partial to working with wood, and named their firm with the Japanese word for 'ash tree'.

www.tonerico-inc.com

Torafu Architects

The Tokyo-based practice was founded in 2004 by Koichi Suzuno and Shinya Kamuro. Suzuno (born in Kanagawa Prefecture in 1973) studied architecture at Tokyo University of Science and received his master's degree from Yokohama National University. Before co-founding Torafu Architects he worked for the architectural office Coelacanth K&H in Tokyo, and then for firms in Australia for three years. Kamuro (born in Shimane

Prefecture in 1974) received both his undergraduate and master's degrees in architecture from Tokyo's Meiji University. Before co-founding Torafu he worked for the architectural firm Jun Aoki & Associates for three years.

www.torafu.com

Hironao Tsuboi // Hironao Tsuboi Design

Tsuboi (born in Tokyo in 1980) studied environmental design at Tokyo's Tama Art University, then followed the advice of his father, who runs a Buddhist temple in Shimoda, and underwent rigorously ascetic Buddhist training for a year. He then worked for an architectural model-maker for more than a year, and in 2005 established the design marketing firm 100% with his older brother, Nobukuni. Together they produced a wide range of products, including housewares, electrical goods and lighting fixtures. Although 100% continues to market his products, in 2010 Tsuboi formed his own independent design firm.

www.hironao-tsuboi.com

Kazuhiro Tsukahara

Tsukahara (born in Kumamoto City in 1957), a member of the design department of the leading stationery producer RayMay Fujii, has been fond of drawing since childhood. He studied law at Tokyo's Komazawa University, but did not choose a legal career, nor did he train as a designer. He joined RayMay Fujii's Tokyo branch in 1981, and has designed many of the company's most successful lines of notebooks and other desk implements. RayMay Fujii was founded in 1890 in Kumamoto City. It opened its Tokyo branch in 1953 and has been making school supplies since 1973.

www.raymay.co.jp

Satoshi Umeno // Umenodesign

Umeno (born in Fukuoka in 1978) initially planned to follow his father's lead and become a carpenter. However, after studying architecture at a local college he began working on shopping-mall projects. Yet the desire to work on smaller projects remained strong, and eventually, after poring over interiors magazines,

Umeno decided to leave Fukuoka and to switch his focus. For the next four years he worked for a furniture-maker in Tokyo, designing living-room pieces and dining tables. In 2003 he launched his own practice with the design and production of *Whale*, an upholstered seating system.

www.umenodesign.com

Un-do Design

Kyoto-based Un-do Design is a partnership founded in 2008 between Rui Matsuo (born in 1983 in Nagasaki) and Yasutaka Kimura (born in 1982 in Kyoto). The designers met as students at Kyoto University of Art and Design, where they both studied space design. Matsuo then began working at a promotional-goods company and Kimura at a furniture fabricator, both in Kyoto. Eager to pursue their own design work without giving up their jobs, the two launched Un-do Design with the intention of creating products that with humour and wit 'undo' preconceived notions.

www.undo-design.com

Hiroaki Watanabe // Plane

Watanabe (born in Fukui Prefecture in 1960) studied industrial design at Tokyo's Kuwasawa Design School. He then joined the Ricoh corporation, where he worked on information-technology equipment, and later moved to Frog Design. After designing audio-visual equipment and optical instruments at the firm's Tokyo office, he transferred to the California office. He left Frog in 1993 for Ziba Design, where he worked until returning to Japan in 1995 and starting his own firm. His company's name, Plane, is taken from his philosophy that design is not about decoration but instead entails planing away the unnecessary.

www.plane-id.co.jp

Kazuhiro Yajima // Kazuhiro Yajima Architect

Yajima (born in Saitama Prefecture in 1976) studied architecture at Tokyo's Hosei University, then went to Stuttgart, Germany, for further architectural study. He returned to Japan after his parents asked him to design their house. 'My mentor told me "Le Corbusier and Venturi both built houses for their parents, so you should, too''', he says. For his parents' house, which occupies a long, thin plot that resulted from the division of a rice paddy, he used roofs of various angles and heights to distinguish the spaces inside.

www.kyarchitect.info

Yamaha

The Yamaha corporation (founded in 1887 by Torakasu Yamaha as Nippon Gakki) started out by making reed organs but grew into the world's largest manufacturer of a full line of musical instruments. 'I have to confess, I don't play any kind of instrument', says Manabu Kawada, general manager of Yamaha's Product Design Laboratory, but he oversees the development of some 300 pianos, drums, stringed instruments and a multitude of other items each year. Each of his twenty-five designers works in teams with engineers and musicians at Yamaha headquarters in Hamamatsu, and follows projects from initial concept to final packaging.

www.yamaha.com

Hideo Yamamoto // Ottimo Design

Yamamoto (born in Tokyo in 1957) once dreamed of becoming a painter, but practical concerns led him to study product design at Tokyo's Tama Art University instead. 'It combined my interests and enabled me to make a living, too', he explains. He then worked in-house for five years at the Yamaha corporation, where he concentrated on interior products but also dabbled in musical equipment, the company's main interest. In 1989 he opened his own firm, Ottimo Design (from the Italian for 'the best'), which creates a wide range of household and interior goods.

www.ottimo-d.com

Mamoru Yasukuni // Kikuchi-Yasukuni Architects

Yasukuni (born in Osaka in 1968) spent his formative years in Niigata City. After studying art history at Tokyo's Waseda University he worked for a small publishing company specializing in maps, and in his spare time began designing *Notchless*.

He quit his job in 2009 and opened his own firm with his wife, an architect with an existing practice. *Notchless* is their first industrial-design product.

www.kikuchi-yasukuni.co.jp

Itaru Yonenaga // No Control Air

Yonenaga (born in Kyoto in 1975) was interested in fashion from a young age, and after studying architecture at Kyoto Seika University hoped to get a job in the clothing industry. Instead he began designing and making clothes independently while holding part-time jobs. In 2000 he and his wife-cum-business partner, Mie, launched No Control Air by self-exhibiting their first line of shirts and dresses to invited buyers. Their Tou line, a collection of innovative knitted accessories that challenge convention, was launched in 2007.

http://nocontrolair.com

Tokujin Yoshioka

Yoshioka (born in Saga Prefecture in 1967) knew from the age of six that he wanted to be a designer. He studied design at Tokyo's Kuwasawa Design School, then worked for the renowned product designer Shiro Kuramata for a year, and for the fashion designer Issey Miyake for four years. He went freelance in 1992 and established his own office in 2000. He continues to collaborate with Issey Miyake on shop designs and exhibition installations.

www.tokujin.com

Yuruliku

The design duo of Koushi Ikegami and Kinue Oneda named their company in 2005 with a made-up blend of the words meaning 'slowly' and 'relax'. Ikegami (born in Fukui Prefecture in 1970) studied product design at the Kyoto Institute of Technology; Oneda (born in Kanagawa Prefecture in 1969) studied printmaking at Tokyo's Joshibi University of Art and Design. The two met while working at a car-upholstery company in Fukui Prefecture. Oneda then worked as a greetings-card designer. To broaden his skills, Ikegami took bag-making classes in his spare time. Yuruliku pools their talents.

www.yuruliku.com

FURTHER READING

Andrew Davey, *Detail: Exceptional Japanese Product Design,* London (Laurence King) 2003

Joachim Fischer, *Young Asian Designers*, Cologne, London and New York (Daab) 2005

Naoto Fukasawa, ed., *Naoto Fukasawa*, London (Phaidon) 2007

Naoto Fukasawa with Tamotsu Fujii, *The Outline*, Tokyo (Hachette Fujingaho) 2009

Shu Hagiwara, *Origins: The Creative Spark Behind Japan's Best Product Designs*, New York (Kodansha) 2006

Kenya Hara, *Designing Design,* Baden (Lars Müller) 2007

—, *Haptic,* Tokyo (Asahi Shimbun) 2004

Japanese Design: A Survey Since 1950, exhib. cat. ed. Kathryn B. Hiesinger and Felice Fischer, Philadelphia Museum of Art, September–November 1994

Masaaki Kanai et al., *Muji*, New York (Rizzoli) 2010

Noriko Kawakami, *Realising Design*, Tokyo (Toto Shuppan) 2004

Sarah Lonsdale, *Japanese Design*, London (Carlton) 2001

Lesley Millar, ed., *2121: The Textile Vision of Reiko Sudo and Nuno,* Canterbury (University College for the Creative Arts) 2005

Ryu Niimi, *Tokujin Yoshioka: Design*, London (Phaidon) 2006

Naomi Pollock, *Modern Japanese House*, London (Phaidon) 2005

Penny Sparke, *Japanese Design*, New York (The Museum of Modern Art) 2009

Shigeru Uchida, *Japanese Interior Design: Its Cultural Origin,* Tokyo (Uchida Design) 2007

Wa: The Spirit of Harmony and Japanese Design Today, exhib. cat. by Hiroshi Kashiwagi et al., Paris, Budapest, Essen, Warsaw, St Étienne and Seoul, 2008–2010

ACKNOWLEDGEMENTS   PICTURE CREDITS

I could not have completed *Made in Japan* without the help and support of many people along the way. First I should like to thank Hugh Merrell and Claire Chandler at Merrell Publishers for commissioning this book. I am very grateful to Marion Moisy, Alex Coco, Nick Wheldon and all the other Merrell members who helped to make it a reality. Their dedication and commitment throughout the process were invaluable to me.

I also wish to thank the many product designers whose works and words are included in the book. I am continually amazed by their ingenuity, enthusiasm and meticulous attention to detail. Their input and willingness to participate made this book possible.

In addition, I should like to thank my mother, Beverly Pollock, for exposing me to good design from a young age. I know that she would have enjoyed this book. I am very grateful to my sister, Beth Ungar, for her unflagging support whenever I need it.

Lastly, I am deeply appreciative of all the encouragement, help and humour provided by my family. It is with great pleasure that I dedicate this book to Abby, Eve and, most of all, David.

Naomi Pollock,

Tokyo, 2012

Jacket, front: Alexandre Coco. **Jacket, back**: H-Concept Co., Ltd. **Page 1**: F1 Colour Ltd. **p. 2**: Yuichi Yamaguchi. **p. 8**: Taniguchi Tomonori. **p. 9**, top: Teradadesign; bottom: Takata Lemnos. **p. 10**, top: SAV/Alamy; centre: Naomi Pollock; bottom: Jeremy Sutton-Hibbert/Alamy. **p. 11**: FantasticJapan/Alamy. **p. 12**: Jeremy Sutton-Hibbert/Alamy. **p. 13**: Pictures From History. **p. 14**: Elizabeth Whiting & Associates/Alamy. **p. 16**: Robert Harding Picture Library/Alamy. **p. 17**: The Museum of Modern Art, New York/Scala Florence. **p. 18**: Muji/Ryouhin Keikaku Co. Ltd. **p. 19**: Hidetoyo Sasaki. **p. 21**: Nobuhiro Sato. **p. 22**: TNA Design Studio. **p. 23**: Naruse Inokuma Architects. **pp. 24–25**: as individual product entries below (unless otherwise indicated).

15.0% pp. 26, 27: Teradadesign Architects/Takata Lemnos. **Acure** p. 29: Nacasa & Partners. **Ai Walk** p. 31: Takano Co. Ltd. **Airvase** pp. 24 (row 1, col. 4), 33: Fuminari Yoshitsugu; p. 32: Satomi Tomita. **Allround Bowls** p. 35: Miyagi Design Office/Cherry Terrace. **Altar for One God** pp. 24 (row 2, col. 1), 37: Seiji Himeno; p. 36: Toshihiko Sakai. **Amorfo Premium** pp. 38, 39: Masahi Ono. **AP Stool** p. 40: sketch model Ryo Kaikura; pp. 40, 41: photographs Luciano Sveliado. **Aquarium Dumbbell** pp. 42, 43: Sumikawa Design/Takenaka Bronze Works. **Bind** p. 45: Satoshi Umeno/Umenodesign. **Bird Alarm Clock** pp. 46, 47: Idea International. **Bottle** pp. 48, 49: Sachiko Suzuki. **Bucket** pp. 50, 51: Idea International. **Carved** p. 53: Takata Lemnos. **CD Player** p. 55: Hidetoyo Sasaki. **Cement Push Pin** p. 57: Nobuhiro Sato. **Chibion Touch** p. 59: Satoshi Nakagawa/Tripod Design. **Conof. Shredder** p. 61: Color/Silver Seiko. **Cook One** p. 63: Hideo Yamamoto. **Cooki** p. 65: IDK Design Laboratory/Stile Life. **Edokomon** p. 67: Nikko Company. **F,l,o,w,e,r,s** p. 69: Norihiko Terayama/Studio Note. **Felt Hook** pp. 70, 71: Junya Sakaguchi. **Fujiyama Glass** p. 73: Keita Suzuki/Sugahara Glassworks. **Guh** p. 75: Iwatani Materials. **Hands** p. 24 (row 6, col. 1): Satoshi Asakawa; p. 77 Kentaro Kamata. **Hanger Tree** pp. 78, 79: Un-do Design. **Higashiya Monaka** p. 81: Shinichiro Ogata/Simplicity. **Hiroshima Arm Chair** p. 83: Yoneo Kawabe. **HK Gravity Pearls** pp. 84, 85: Eisuke Tachikawa/Nosigner. **Honey-comb Mesh + Bracelet** pp. 86, 87: Seiji Oguri. **Honeycomb Lamp** p. 89: Yuichi Yamaguchi. **Humidifier** p. 91: Hidetoyo Sasaki. **Infobar A01** p. 93: KDDI/Naoto Fukasawa. **Ishikoro** p. 95: Yoshii Towel Company. **Kadokeshi** p. 97: Barakan Design. **Kai Table** p. 99: Takumi Ota Photography. **Kamikirimushi** p. 101: Satoshi Nakagawa/Tripod Design. **Kibiso Sandals** p. 103: Keiko Matsubara. **Kinoishi** p. 105: Taku Satoh Design Office. **Knot** pp. 106, 107: Shigeki Fujishiro. **Kudamemo** p. 109: D-Bros/Draft. **Kulms Chair** p. 111: Lerival LLP. **Lucano** pp. 112, 113: Metaphys/Hasegawa Kogyo. **Many Heels** pp. 114, 115: No Control Air. **Megaphone** p. 117: Ryo Kaikura. **Melte** pp. 118, 119: Atsushi Yamauchi/Honda Keigo Design. **Mindbike** p. 121: TSDesign Ltd. **Mizusashi** p. 123: Taniguchi Tomonori. **Moka Knives** pp. 124, 125: Kawashi

Design Room/Kawashima Industry. **Monacca** p. 127: Taniguchi Tomonori. **Nekko** pp. 128, 129: H-Concept Co., Ltd. **Nook** pp. 130, 131: Yusuke Miyake. **Noon** p. 133: Yukichi Anno. **Notchless** pp. 134, 135: Kikuchi-Yasukuni Architects. **Number Cup** pp. 136, 137: H-Concept Co., Ltd. **Number Measuring Spoons** p. 139: Atsuhiro Hayashi. **Oishi Kitchen Table** p. 141: Nacasa & Partners. **Ojue** pp. 142, 143: Metaphys/Cube Egg. **One For All** pp. 144, 145: Naruse Inokuma Architects/Sumitomo Forestry. **Paper-Wood** pp. 25 (row 3, col. 1), 146: Drill Design; p. 147: Takumi Ota Photography. **Pencut** pp. 148, 149: RayMay Fujii. **Plugo** p. 151: Itsuo Sato/Masayuki Kurakata. **Pokehashi** p. 153: Cube Egg. **Reconstruction Chandelier** p. 155: Yuichi Yamaguchi. **Red & Blue** pp. 156, 157: Yuruliku. **Retto** pp. 158, 159: Iwatani Materials. **Ripples** pp. 160, 161: Gianni Antoniali/Ikon. **Rock** p. 163: Takumi Ota. **Roll** pp. 164, 165: Nendo/Flaminia. **Round & Round** pp. 166, 167: Shunsuke Takahashi. **Sakurasaku** p. 169: Hironao Tsuboi. **Sen** p. 171: Pinto. **Silent Guitar** p. 173: Yamaha. **Skip** pp. 174, 175: C.H.O. Design. **Sleepy** p. 176: illustration by Noritake; p. 177: Takafumi Yamada. **Soft Dome Slide** p. 179: Nacasa & Partners. **Spin** p. 181: Sakai Design. **Splash** pp. 182, 183: H-Concept Co., Ltd. **Stand** pp. 184, 185: Genta Design/Duende. **Standing Rice Scoop** pp. 25 (row 7, col. 1), 240: F1 Colour Ltd.; pp. 186, 187: Marna. **Step Step** p. 189: Kawakami Design Room/Nissin Furniture Crafters. **Suspence** p. 191: Naoko Ishibashi. **Tatamiza** pp. 192, 193: Hara Design Institute/Hida Sangyo. **Thin Black Lines Chair** p. 195: Masayuki Hayashi. **Tiggy** p. 197: Sue McNab. **Till** p. 199: Duende. **Toaster** p. 201: Hidetoyo Sasaki. **Tsuzumi** p. 203: Studio Gen. **Tubelumi** p. 205: Plane/Nissho Telecom. **Twelve** p. 207: Naoto Fukasawa/Seiko Instruments. **Twiggy** p. 209: Maxray. **Two Piece** p. 210: Drill Design/Mizutori. **Umbrella Tea House** p. 25 (row 9, col. 4): drawing by Kazuhiro Yajima Architect; pp. 212, 213: Satoshi Shigeta/Nacasa & Partners. **Wasara** pp. 214, 215: Shinichiro Ogata/Simplicity/Wasara Co., Ltd. **Whill** p. 216: Satoshi Sugie. **X-Ray** pp. 218, 219: Tokujin Yoshioka Inc. **Yama** p. 220: drawing by Mikiya Kobayashi Design; p. 221: Yosuke Owashi. **Yu Wa I** p. 222: drawing by Architecture + Interior Design Issun; p. 223: Ken Fujiyama. **Zutto Rice Cooker** p. 225: Koji Miura.

The publisher has made every effort to trace and contact copyright holders of the material reproduced in this book. It will be happy to correct in subsequent editions any errors or omissions that are brought to its attention.

INDEX

NAOMI POLLOCK is an American architect based in Japan. Her writing on Japanese design has appeared in the *Financial Times*, *New York Times*, *Wallpaper** and *Architectural Record*. She is the author of *Modern Japanese House* (2005) and *Hitoshi Abe* (2008), and co-author of Merrell's *New Architecture in Japan* (2010).

REIKO SUDO is Artistic Director of the award-winning avant-garde textile company Nuno Corporation.

First published 2012 by
Merrell Publishers, London and New York

Merrell Publishers Limited
81 Southwark Street
London SE1 0HX

merrellpublishers.com

Text copyright © 2012 Naomi Pollock
Illustrations copyright © 2012 the copyright holders;
    see page 236
Design and layout copyright © 2012 Merrell
    Publishers Limited

All rights reserved. No part of this publication may be reproduced, stored in a retrieval system or transmitted, in any form or by any means, electronic, mechanical, photocopying, recording or otherwise, without the prior written permission of the publisher.

British Library Cataloguing-in-Publication Data:
Pollock, Naomi R.
Made in Japan: 100 new products.
1. Industrial design–Japan–History–21st century.
2. New products–Japan–History–21st century.
I. Title
745.2'0952-dc23

ISBN 978-1-8589-4562-0

Produced by Merrell Publishers Limited
Designed by Alexandre Coco
Project-managed by Marion Moisy
Indexed by Hilary Bird

Printed and bound in China

The foreword was translated from the Japanese by Alfred Birnbaum.

Front cover, page 1 and below
Standing Rice Scoop; see page 186

Back cover
Splash umbrella stand; see page 182

Page 2
Reconstruction Chandelier; see page 154

Pages 24–25
The 100 products featured in this book (pages 26–225), shown in order of appearance